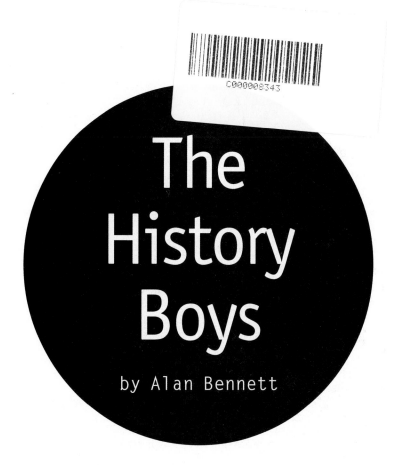

The History Boys

by Alan Bennett

Authors and Series Editors:
Sue Bennett and Dave Stockwin

HODDER
EDUCATION
AN HACHETTE UK COMPANY

The publisher would like to thank the following for permission to reproduce copyright material:

Acknowledgments:

pp. 8, 9 Telegraph Media Group Limited 2004; **pp. 13, 32, 44, 58** Guardian News & Media Ltd 2015; **p. 49** Maurice Rutherford (quotation cited from http://philiplarkin.com/poem-reviews/mcmxiv). Excerpts from *The History Boys* by permission of Faber and Faber Ltd.

Photo credits:

p. 8 TopFoto; **p. 9** Bentley Archive/Popperfoto/Getty Images; **p. 18** Tony Baggett/Fotolia; **p. 19** AF archive/Alamy; **pp. 31, 32** Snap Stills/Rex; **p. 43** Michal Miasko/Fotolia; **p. 62** Everett Collection/Rex

Orders: please contact Bookpoint Ltd, 130 Park Drive, Milton Park, Abingdon, Oxon OX14 4SE. Telephone: (44) 01235 827720. Fax: (44) 01235 400454. Lines are open 9.00–17.00, Monday to Saturday, with a 24-hour message answering service. Visit our website at www.hoddereducation.co.uk

First published in 2016 by

Hodder Education

An Hachette UK Company,

Carmelite House, 50 Victoria Embankment

London EC4Y 0LS

Impression number		5	4	3	2	
Year	2020	2019	2018	2017	2016	

Cover photo Necip Yanmaz/iStockphoto

Typeset in 11/13pt Bliss Light by Integra Software Services Pvt. Ltd., Pondicherry, India

Printed in Dubai

A catalogue record for this title is available from the British Library

ISBN 9781471853678

Contents

This guide is designed to help you to raise your achievement in your examination response to *The History Boys*. It is intended for you to use throughout your GCSE English literature course. It will help you when you are studying the play for the first time and also during your revision.

The following features have been used throughout this guide to help you focus your understanding of the play:

Target your thinking

A list of **introductory questions** labelled by Assessment Objective is provided at the beginning of each chapter to give you a breakdown of the material covered. They target your thinking in order to help you work more efficiently by focusing on the key messages.

Build critical skills

These offer an opportunity to consider some more challenging questions. They are designed to encourage deeper thinking, analysis and exploratory thought. Building and practising critical skills in this way will give you a real advantage in the examination.

GRADE *FOCUS*

It is possible to know a play well and yet still underachieve in the examination if you are unsure of what the examiners are looking for. The **GRADE FOCUS** boxes give a clear explanation of how you may be assessed, with an emphasis on the criteria for gaining a Grade 5 and a Grade 8.

REVIEW YOUR LEARNING

At the end of each chapter you will find the **Review your learning** section to test your knowledge: a series of short specific questions to ensure that you have understood and absorbed the key messages of the section. Answers to the Review your learning questions are provided in the final section of the guide (p.102).

GRADE *BOOSTER*

Read and remember this grade-boosting advice: top tips from experienced teachers and examiners who can advise you on what to do, as well as what not to do, to maximise your chances of success in the examination.

Key quotation

Hector *...remember, open quotation marks, 'All knowledge is precious whether or not it serves the slightest human use', close quotation marks. (p. 5)*

Key quotations are highlighted for you, so that if you wish you may use them as **supporting evidence** in your examination answers. Further quotations grouped by characterisation, key moments and theme can be found in the Top ten quotations section towards the end of the guide. Page references are given for the 2004 Faber and Faber edition of the text.

Studying the text

You may find it useful to read sections of this guide when you need them, rather than reading it from start to finish. For example, the section on Context can be read before you read the play itself, since it offers an explanation of relevant historical, cultural and literary background to the text. It is here where you will find information on aspects of Bennett's life which influenced his writing, the particular issues with which Bennett was concerned and on where the play stands in terms of the literary tradition to which it belongs.

As you work through the play, you may find it helpful to read the plot and structure sections before or after reading a particular Act or section of text. As well as a summary of events there is also commentary, so that you are aware of key events and features in each of the sections. The sections on characterisation, themes, and language, style and analysis, will help to develop your thinking further, in preparation for written responses on particular aspects of the text.

Many students also enjoy the experience of being able to bring something extra to their classroom lessons in order to be 'a step ahead of the game'. Alternatively, you may have missed a classroom session or feel that you need a clearer explanation and the guide can help you with this too.

An initial reading of the section on Assessment Objectives and skills will enable you to make really effective notes in preparation for assessments. The Assessment Objectives are what examination boards base their mark schemes on. In this section they are broken down and clearly explained.

Revising the text

Whether you study the play in a block of time close to the exam or much earlier in your GCSE literature course, you will need to revise thoroughly if you are to achieve the very best grade that you can.

You should first remind yourself of what happens in the play and so the chapter on plot and structure might be returned to in the first instance. You might then look at the Assessment Objectives section to ensure that you understand what the examiners are looking for in general, and then look carefully at the Tackling the exams section.

This section gives you useful information on question format, depending on which examination board specification you are following, as well as practical advice on the examination format, and practical considerations such as the time available for the question and the Assessment

Objectives which apply to it. There is advice on how to approach the question, writing a quick plan, and beginning your response.

Focused advice on how to raise your grade follows, and you need to read this section carefully.

You will also find examples of exam-style responses in the Sample essays section, with examiners' comments in the margins, so that you can see clearly how to move towards a Grade 5 and how to then move from Grade 5 to Grade 8. Further exam board-specific questions are available in the online resources.

Now that all GCSE literature examinations are 'closed book', the Top ten section will be an invaluable aid in that it offers you the opportunity to learn short quotations to support points about character and themes.

When writing about the play, use this guide as a springboard to develop your own ideas. Remember: the examiners are not looking for set responses. You should not read this guide in order to memorise chunks of it, ready to regurgitate in the exam. Identical answers are dull. The examiners hope to reward you for perceptive thought, individual appreciation and varying interpretations. They want to sense you have engaged with the themes and ideas in the play, explored Bennett's methods with an awareness of the context in which he wrote and enjoyed this part of your literature course.

The play in performance

If you are fortunate enough to be offered the opportunity to see the play on stage, this would be most useful to deepen your understanding of it. There is also an enjoyable film version of *The History Boys* (2006) which will help to familiarise you with the main characters and bring the play to life, especially through the use of song and the pacey style.

However, there are some important differences between the play and the film. For instance, the play is much darker in terms of the ending; in the film, a more sympathetically portrayed Irwin has suffered nothing more than a broken leg in the accident. Posner too seems brighter in the film — 'not happy but not unhappy about it', rather than the reclusive, neurotic figure from the play.

It is important to remember that your examination is on the play, not on the film.

Enjoy referring to the guide, and good luck in your exam.

Target your thinking

- What is meant by 'context'? (**AO3**)
- How has Bennett's early life influenced his work? (**AO3**)
- How is the context of the 1980s reflected in *The History Boys*? (**AO3**)
- What is the literary context of the play? (**AO3**)
- How does Bennett evoke a wider cultural context? (**AO3**)

What is context?

Knowledge of context will help you to understand and appreciate your reading of *The History Boys*, but what exactly is it?

'Context' is a wide-ranging term. It refers to the historical, socioeconomic and political circumstances of the time, as well as the author's beliefs about those circumstances. It also refers to the way that more personal events in the life of the author (in this case Alan Bennett) may have influenced his/her thinking and writing. Finally, it may also refer to literary context and be concerned with developments in the play as a form which may also have influenced the way it was written.

▲ Alan Bennett

Bennett and *The History Boys*

Alan Bennett was born in Leeds in 1934 into a working-class family. He attended a state grammar school which was in many ways similar to the school in *The History Boys*. He was taught history by a teacher who he later described as being closest to Mrs Lintott, with a solid, factual approach to teaching.

He has expressed some regret that he was never taught by anyone like the charismatic and inspirational Hector. As he explains in an interview in the *Daily Telegraph*, 21 June 2004:

'I only knew about teachers like that from talking to other people, and also from reading…Temperamentally I cleave to that kind of teacher and that kind of teaching — while at the same time not thinking it practical.'

He was one of eight boys in his sixth form who were encouraged by the Head to try for one of the more prestigious universities. At that time, candidates went up to Cambridge or Oxford for an interview and to sit the entrance examination, and Bennett found this adventure both exciting and intimidating. Some of his feelings regarding this period of his life inevitably informed his portrayal of the experiences of the boys in the play.

After completing his National Service, he decided to try for a scholarship to Oxford, partly from 'sheer vanity' but also because, like Posner, he'd fallen hopelessly in love with a boy who was going there. Later he came to regret the journalistic approach to history that he used, albeit successfully, to gain his place there.

> '...the way I got a scholarship to Oxford and how I got my degree really was via the method the character called Irwin uses in the play. So in a sense, I am Irwin.' (*Daily Telegraph*, 21 June 2004)

However, he also sees himself in other characters, such as the religious Scripps and the undersized Posner, who is coming to terms with his emerging sexuality. In fact, Bennett has commented:

> 'I'm all the boys except for Dakin, the most confident boy. I wish I could, but I can't see myself in him. And the masters too. I think all dramatists work like that. There's a pinch of you in every character.' (*Daily Telegraph*, 21 June 2004)

During his time at university he became involved with the **Oxford Revue** and was also part of a group which went to the Edinburgh Festival with the highly successful satirical show *Beyond the Fringe*. This led to work in television and ultimately to various other writing projects. His other most well-known work includes the *Talking Heads* series, *The Lady in the Van* and *The Madness of King George*.

In his autobiographical essays he refers to the 'futile filthy deaths of war' and he also marched in protest at the war in Iraq, which he regarded as 'shameful'. His abhorrence of war is reflected in the empathy shown by Hector and Posner for the fate of Drummer Hodge in Thomas Hardy's poem of the same name.

His views on history may possibly be close to those of Mrs Lintott since he has also expressed disgust over populist interpretations of Henry VIII and the dissolution of the monasteries. This disgust informs his scathing portrayal of Irwin as a television celebrity historian.

Oxford Revue: comedy group featuring Oxford University students which also produced Rowan Atkinson, Michael Palin and Katy Brand

▲ The cast of *Beyond the Fringe*, 1962 (with Alan Bennett on the right)

GRADE BOOSTER

It is important to have some knowledge of the author's life as well as the context of the play. This will help you to understand the author's purposes and concerns as well as any contemporary issues which may have affected the presentation of characters or themes. However, there is little to be gained by simply 'bolting on' biographical or cultural details. They must always be related to the question you are answering.

The 1980s

Although the play first premièred in 2004, it is loosely set in the 1980s. When Bennett was writing the play in the early 2000s, he would have had time to reflect on some of the major events of that era, a time when the educational *zeitgeist* was undergoing massive change, prompting similar debates about the nature and purpose of education to those in the play. In addition, central government began to establish a tighter control over schools, colleges and universities than ever before.

zeitgeist: the spirit of the age or time

Universities in the 1980s

The Conservative government, under Margaret Thatcher, argued that universities should be brought closer to the world of business. This meant greater exposure to market forces, increased monitoring and massive cuts in spending. Education for its own sake was, apparently, considered of less value than the production of leaders and manpower for business and industry. The treatment of universities was compared by a London professor, John Griffith of the LSE, to Henry VIII's dissolution of the monasteries.

Then, as now, students from state schools were under-represented at **Oxbridge**. Top jobs are dominated by privately educated Oxbridge graduates. In August 2014 the *Independent* reported that 59% of the Cabinet had been to Oxbridge.

Oxbridge: a shorthand term for Oxford or Cambridge

In the play, Irwin knows that Oxbridge places were largely won by wealthier, privately educated students; the kind of young people 'who have been to Rome and Venice, Florence and Perugia and...done courses on what they have seen there' (p. 19). Irwin exhorts the boys to take these young people on:

Key quotation

Irwin *Hate them because these boys and girls...have been groomed like thoroughbreds for this one particular race. Put head to head with them and, on the evidence of these essays, you have none of you got a hope. (p. 20)*

The suggestion is that young people who are privately educated have a veneer of confidence, perhaps what the Headmaster thinks of as 'polish'. They tend to go on to be successful in every sphere of business and professional life. Many prominent figures in the Arts have been privately educated, for example, Eddie Redmayne, Benedict Cumberbatch, Florence Welch, Mumford and Sons, to name but a few.

Bennett has stated publicly his 'passionate view' that state and private education should be amalgamated, especially at sixth form level. Although Irwin appears superficial and in many ways deeply cynical, it could also be argued that Irwin's teaching methods were simply creating a more level playing field for those not from public school backgrounds.

Schools in the 1980s

In the introduction to the Faber edition of *The History Boys*, Bennett tells us that the play is set in a state grammar school. In other words, it is a secondary school where students are selected on ability, as opposed to a comprehensive school which accepts all students regardless of ability. The fact that it is a state school, however, means that it is free for students to attend.

In state schools in the 1980s, the national curriculum was introduced. This prescribed what was to be taught and backed it up with a rigorous system of testing. Teachers were no longer trusted to determine the content of what they taught. In this sense, Irwin was correct when he said that there was no longer time for Hector's inspirational but unregulated approach to teaching.

The publication of league tables based on examination success was also introduced around this time. These work a little like football league tables with the schools with the highest percentage of examination passes at the top (as opposed to the highest number of points gained in matches). The Headmaster in the play cites league tables as one of the reasons he wants the boys to go to Oxbridge.

Many parents felt that the introduction of the publication of league tables had some benefits, in that schools were accountable for their students' results in a way that they had never been before. Furthermore, parents could now, in theory at least, exercise choice over the school their child attended, based on the greater availability of information.

However, there were some less positive effects. To ensure continued existence, schools needed to compete for students as each student brought an increase in funding. As parents inevitably chose schools which were successful according to this one crude measure, many schools felt pressurised to produce results through cramming, or like Irwin, teaching to a particular kind of test, often at the expense of a more rounded education.

In *The History Boys*, Bennett examines the tension between these two different approaches, both philosophically and in practical terms.

Key quotation

Irwin *He was a good man but I do not think there is time for his kind of teaching any more. (p. 109)*

Key quotation

Headmaster *But I am thinking league tables. Open scholarships. Reports to the Governors. (p. 8)*

Contemporary attitudes to sexuality

There were also changes in attitudes to sexuality. Homosexual activity had been illegal in England until 1967, after which homosexual activity between two consenting adults aged 21 was legalised. This was the case at the time in which the play was set. The age of consent for gay men was not reduced to 18 until 1994 and it was only in 2001 that it was equalised to 16, regardless of orientation. Thus, Bennett was writing in a time when attitudes to homosexuality in England were more liberal than those of the time in which the play was set. In fact, the 1980s had seen a toughening of attitudes and a rise in homophobia due to the vast amount of misinformation and panic generated by the first cases of AIDS.

A piece of government legislation, Section 28, was introduced in 1988 which prohibited any teaching which might be seen to promote homosexuality, and its many opponents saw this piece of legislation as highly offensive, as it created an atmosphere of distrust and paranoia which meant that many teachers, like Irwin, were unable to be honest about their sexuality.

In the play, of the three homosexual characters, only Posner is openly gay, although he clearly states that he believes it is one of the reasons his life will not be easy.

As his portrayal of Hector is generally sympathetic, Bennett has been challenged over the notion of Hector's abuse of the boys. He appears relaxed about it, arguing that the boys would have been 17 or 18, and went with Hector quite willingly. Nor do they appear to have been damaged by the experience, and there is a comedic element to the idea that the abuse took place on the back of a motorbike. However, it is an issue about which many modern audience members feel uncomfortable, particularly since there have been a number of high profile scandals in recent years involving sexual activity between adults and youngsters. At the very least, most audience members would agree that Hector's behaviour represents a clear abuse of power. Relationships between teachers and students under 18 were outlawed in 2003.

Literary context

This refers to the position of the play within the genre and the way that other literary works or conventions may have influenced the writer. Although some audiences would probably describe *The History Boys* as simply a comedy, the play is actually rather difficult to categorise as it cleverly mixes comedy and drama, addressing serious issues such as education and history, while also using poetry, music and frequent allusions to both 'high' and 'low' culture.

The History Boys, despite some of the unrealistically elegant speech of the boys, could be said to contain some aspects of naturalistic and realistic drama, movements which developed in the mid to late nineteenth century, in that the audience is clearly expected to care about the lives of characters such as Hector and Posner, and would be expected to identify with situations in the play. There are also times when the characters use natural speech patterns and simple, everyday vocabulary.

However, the play also owes much to the techniques of epic theatre, a movement associated with the German playwright, Bertolt Brecht, in the 1930s. For example, Bennett plays with notions of time, utilising flash-forwards (as in the opening sections of each Act) and including moments where characters seem to step outside of time and speak directly to the audience in the past tense as Timms does early in Act One: 'The hitting never hurt. It was a joke. None of us cared. We lapped it up' (p. 7). This method of directly addressing the audience, or what is termed 'breaking the fourth wall', occurs to comic effect when Mrs Lintott observes that she has 'not hitherto been allotted an inner voice' (p. 68) a **metatheatrical** interruption which goes against the conventions of realistic or naturalistic theatre.

> metatheatrical: a direct reference to a theatre convention by an actor which reminds the audience that they are watching a play

For further discussion of 'breaking the fourth wall', turn to p. 55 in the Language, style and analysis section.

In addition, it is unlikely that the boys, although bright, would have the breadth of knowledge that they display. The acceptance of Posner's homosexuality in a state grammar school in the 1980s is perhaps unlikely too, and both Hector and Irwin symbolise two extreme views. Bennett is not attempting a re-creation of an actual classroom, but rather prioritising drama over realism.

> 'No one actually talks as eloquently as the boys do in the play,' he says, 'but you, hopefully, go along with it because you are willing to suspend disbelief and, within the context of the play, it works. Of course, you hope to make certain points, but what matters most of all is that the audience must be carried along for the duration of the play.' (Alan Bennett, *Guardian*, 17 October 2006)

Cultural context

Cultural context is used here to refer to the effect of the wide range of literary and cultural allusions in the play, from popular culture as well as from poetry, drama, philosophy and so on. Although the play is set in the 1980s, its cultural context is considerably wider. The songs and films are those of Hector's youth; as Rudge says, Hector's 'crap' as opposed to their 'crap,' which is represented by the Pet Shop Boys' recording of 'It's a Sin'. Realistically, even given the boys' admiration for Hector in the early stages of the play, it is unlikely that they would have been familiar with so much earlier popular culture. However, the audience willingly suspend disbelief as songs or film extracts enrich the play, creating humour, drama or pathos.

> **Build critical skills**
>
> The theatre critic Michael Billington described *The History Boys* as 'the most experimental play in London' (*Guardian*, 29 May 2004). In what ways do you think the play is 'experimental'?

intertextuality: a literary device which involves a writer using references to other works in order to add layers of meaning to their own writing. (For more examples of this device see the Intertextuality section in Language, style and analyis on p. 60.)

For example, the fact that Posner is unlikely to have been so familiar with 'Bewitched, Bothered and Bewildered', a 1940 Rogers and Hart classic, as to sing it in the classroom does not matter. As a moving song of love and yearning for Dakin, it adds deep emotional resonance, even more so given that the troubled Lorenz Hart who wrote the lyrics, was, like Posner, small, Jewish and gay.

'Wish Me Luck as You Wave Me Goodbye' is sung by the boys as they leave for Oxbridge. The song was made popular by 'Lancashire lass' Gracie Fields during the Second World War.

The boys' acting out of scenes from popular 1940s films such as *Brief Encounter* or *Now, Voyager* adds humour as well as an awareness of the possible absurdity of the theatrical nature of unhappy love affairs.

The idea that sometimes, in order to fully understand a text, we need to be familiar with other texts is known as '**intertextuality**'. Bennett uses this to greatest effect in the use of poetry. For example, the scene where Posner and Hector discuss Thomas Hardy's 'Drummer Hodge' reveals their own loneliness. Bennett also explains, through Hector, how a knowledge of literature can both inform and comfort readers years later.

This can also be seen in the boys' recital of Philip Larkin's 'MCMXIV'. Layers of time are peeled back to reveal our connection to the past as we watch or read a play in the second decade of the twenty-first century, written in the beginning of that century but set in the 1980s. The boys show an appreciation of a poem written in the 1960s, about a line of men and boys going to war and probable death in 1914.

REVIEW YOUR LEARNING

1 What is meant by the term 'context'?

2 What reasons has Bennett given for trying for a scholarship to Oxford?

3 Why does Bennett link himself with Irwin?

4 Which character does Bennett see none of himself in?

5 When was the play first premièred, and when is it set?

6 What two measures were introduced into schools in the 1980s which changed the educational climate?

7 What was the age of consent between gay men when the play was set?

8 Why might Irwin have been unable to be open about his sexuality?

9 What is meant by the term 'breaking the fourth wall'?

10 Give two examples of 'flash-forwards' in the play.

Answers on p. 102.

Plot and structure

Target your thinking

- What are the main events in the play? (**AO1**)
- What functions are performed by the events within the play? (**AO2**)
- How does Bennett use dramatic structure? (**AO2**)

Structure

The History Boys is a two-Act play. Although the narrative is largely chronological, covering approximately 3 months of action, there are 'flash-forwards' at the openings of each Act. By allowing us a glimpse of Irwin's future both as a 'celebrity historian' and a government '**spin doctor**' at the start of each Act, Bennett enables the audience to see the rise of Irwin's approach both in the media and in politics.

> **spin doctor:** a person who is employed, usually by a political party, to put a favourable 'spin' on events or an unpopular policy

There are also a number of moments when characters 'step out' and seem to address the audience directly, looking back upon the events. This too extends the play's time scope to around 20 years. In addition, the abundance of historical references suggests that 'it moves far beyond the initially restrictive time and space in which it is set, to bind together influences from across the twentieth century and before' (James Middlemarch, *emagazine* 46, December 2009).

Although the play is not formally separated into scenes, and the action seems fluid and seamless, Bennett juxtaposes key events for effect; for example, the lessons of Hector and Irwin are placed consecutively to bring out the contrast in their teaching. Comic scenes contrast with moving moments such as the recital of Philip Larkin's 'MCMXIV' by the boys, after the bell has gone, proving indeed that 'Art wins in the end' (p. 27).

At the same time, the placing of Hector as the final voice in the play gives resonance to his message about the importance of the 'passing on' of knowledge.

In order to make revision more straightforward, the guide divides each Act into accessible sections, often linked by theme or character.

The plot

As already noted, at various times in the play Bennett allows characters to 'step out' from the action and address the audience from some unspecified point in the future. These moments make creating an absolutely accurate timeline very difficult. What follows are two simplified timelines, one showing key events as they are presented on stage and the other putting those events into chronological order.

Act One events

- Irwin, in his forties, is shown as a 'spin doctor'
- Flashback: school, autumn term (around 20 years earlier)
- Preparing the boys for Oxbridge
- Hector's inappropriate behaviour witnessed

Act Two events

- Flash-forward approximately 5 years – Irwin as celebrity historian
- Flashback: school, end of autumn term
- Hector and Irwin's shared lesson
- 'Mock' interviews
- Spring term – success for the boys
- The accident happens
- Hector's memorial service
- Flash-forward: boys look back on Hector/their futures are revealed

▲ 'On stage' timeline of events

- Beginning of autumn term, the 1980s
- Irwin brought in to teach, aged mid-20s
- Hector incident witnessed
- Oxbridge exams take place
- Success for the boys
- The accident happens
- Hector's memorial service
- Irwin, aged 30, shown as celebrity historian
- The boys look back as adults remembering Hector
- Irwin, now in his forties, becomes a political 'spin doctor'

▲ Chronological timeline of events

Act One

- Irwin is seen as a 'spin doctor'
- Hector is introduced as an eccentric teacher
- Head reveals his plan to gain Oxbridge places for the boys
- Head and Irwin interrupt Hector's French lesson
- Scripps does 'pillion duty' with Hector
- Irwin's first lesson — Irwin's 'method' introduced
- Dakin 'seeing' Fiona, the Head's secretary
- Hector's poetry lesson and the first 'film game'
- The boys cross-examine Irwin

- Posner confesses his love of Dakin to Irwin
- Head confronts Hector over motorbike 'activities' and forces him to take retirement to avoid dismissal
- Hector and Posner discuss 'Drummer Hodge' by Thomas Hardy

Section 1: Irwin's future in government (p. 3)

The play opens with a flash-forward, approximately 20 years after the main action of the play. Irwin, now in his forties, is in a wheelchair addressing MPs. He appears to have become a 'spin doctor' in that he is giving advice on how to fool the electorate into accepting an unpopular bill by 'bending the truth', a process which reminds him of school. This brief scene establishes his glib cynicism and willingness to manipulate language to his purposes.

Paradox is a statement that seems to contradict itself, and is sometimes used to make the speaker sound either clever or interesting. Here, Irwin is suggesting that by using a nonsensical paradox, such as 'The loss of liberty is the price we pay for freedom' (p. 1), the politicians can confuse the public so that they are unable to see the truth, and will accept what the politicians say.

Key quotation

Irwin *Paradox works well and mists up the windows, which is handy. (p. 1)*

Section 2: Introducing key characters (pp. 3–12)

The classroom scene which follows gives the general setting of a sixth-form classroom in a boys' school in the north of England in the 1980s. We are introduced to Hector, a teacher in his fifties, and 'his sixth-formers, eight boys of seventeen or eighteen' (p. 1).

Hector arrives in his motorcycle leathers and helmet which the boys ceremoniously remove and present to the audience in French. Stage directions tell us that Hector has an air of 'studied eccentricity' which is confirmed by his first somewhat overblown speech, and perhaps by the stage direction which tells us that he wears a 'bow tie'. We learn that the boys have passed their A-levels and now intend to try for Oxbridge. His despair over their desire to do so is parodied in the scene from *King Lear*, a scene which perhaps foreshadows the death of Hector. It also allows the audience to see that the boys are bright, perceptive and knowledgeable.

King Lear: one of Shakespeare's greatest tragedies where a proud King is driven to madness and death through his ill-treatment by his daughters

Build critical skills

Can you see any other links between the play and *King Lear*? Think about the roles played by Timms and Posner as well as Hector's character.

We also learn that Hector is to teach them general studies which he views as 'A Waste of Time' (p. 5). The rapport between teacher and students is clearly demonstrated; they regard his hitting them as a both a joke and a sign of his affection:

Key quotation

Rudge *He hits you if he likes you. He never touches me.*

Dakin (happily) *I'm black and blue. (p. 7)*

The scene changes to the staffroom where Bennett uses the first appearance of Mrs Lintott and the Headmaster to contrast her sharp intelligence with his snobbery and false values as he reveals his desire for the boys to gain 'polish' in order to get into Oxbridge.

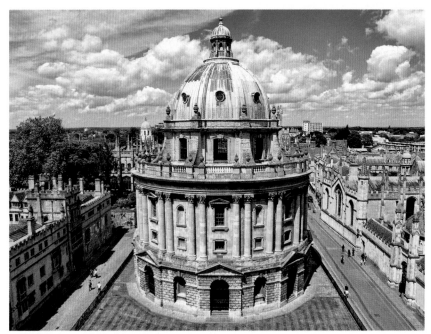

▲ Radcliffe Camera in Oxford

Deflating his notion of 'polish', she exerts a negative influence on the audience's view of the Headmaster. In addition, she appears to support Hector's view that the pursuit of Oxbridge acceptance is not a particularly worthy one, as she undermines the Headmaster's ideas by her references to 'parsley' and 'an umbrella in the cocktail' (p. 9).

Section 3: Comparing Hector and Irwin's teaching styles (pp. 12–27)

Scripps, in his role as occasional narrator, comments on the arrival of the new teacher, Irwin, as 'clandestine' which could be interpreted as a warning to the audience that Irwin may be a somewhat shady character. This time, Irwin is not in a wheelchair, which sets an enigma which is not solved until much later in the play. He is briefed by the Headmaster that his mission is to gain Oxbridge scholarships for the school so that they may rise up the league table.

In Hector's French lesson, the boys improvise an hilarious scene in a French brothel, which, when the Head arrives with Irwin, they explain away as a scene in a wartime hospital.

▲ Dakin: caught with his trousers down in the 2006 film version of the play

This establishes the boys' loyalty to Hector, who, when requested, refuses to give up teaching time to Irwin. This short section also reveals Irwin's breadth of knowledge as he adds the French word for 'shell-shocked' to the improvisation.

After the lesson, Hector offers a lift to any of the boys, although he turns down Posner's offer to accompany him. Scripps reluctantly, but dutifully, accepts.

Irwin hands back the boys' books accusing them of being 'dull', making it clear that he feels the boys have no chance of success in the Oxbridge examinations, and the audience is given a first hint of Irwin's 'method' to achieve success:

Key quotation

Irwin *Of course, there is another way.*

Crowther *How?*

Timms *Cheat?*

Irwin *Possibly. (p. 20)*

After Irwin's first lesson it is clear that the boys are generally unimpressed by their new teacher. Dakin reveals that he is seeing Fiona, the Head's secretary and it becomes clear to the audience that the boys' pillion riding with Hector involves submitting to his highly inappropriate fondling of their genitals. It is suggested that they tolerate this abuse because of their regard for him.

W. H. Auden: poet (1907–73); the reference is to the poem 'Letter to Lord Byron'

General Haig: a largely unpopular First World War general, nicknamed 'Butcher Haig' because of the 2 million lives lost under his command. In the 1980s some historians attempted to restore his reputation

Key quotation

Irwin ...*truth is no more at issue in an examination than thirst at a wine-tasting or fashion at a striptease. (p. 26)*

Larkin: Philip Larkin (1922–85) was a Hull-born poet, much admired by Bennett

Now, Voyager: film made in 1942 — the scene the boys re-enact is a famous one for Hector's generation of film-goers

The conversation which follows in the staffroom between Hector and Mrs Lintott functions as an interlude between Irwin's two lessons. The scene confirms their friendship, as well as Mrs Lintott's down-to-earth approach, particularly in her assessment of Dakin, which, in its use of taboo language, may come as something of a surprise to the audience. She dismisses Hector's liberal but more romantic views that Dakin is 'sad' as well as his endorsement of Auden's idea that a degree of neurosis is good for children.

In the scene featuring Irwin's lesson on the First World War, we see a further demonstration of the Irwin method. He dismisses the war poets as 'bloodthirsty' and invites the students to consider a very different view of General Haig and the causes of the war, calling the conflict a 'mistake... not a tragedy' (p. 26).

The lesson ends with a number of the boys reciting Larkin's moving poem 'MCMIV', a feat which baffles, and perhaps impresses, Irwin, leading him to shout after them: 'Not that it answers the question' (p. 27).

GRADE BOOSTER

```
Remember that a line may be delivered in a number of
ways depending on the effect an actor, or director,
wishes to create. Adopt a tentative style, using words
such as 'might', 'may' and 'could' to show that you
understand this.
```

Section 4: Sex, locked doors and Irwin's view of history (pp. 28–41)

Dakin's somewhat immature attitude to sex is presented through his extended metaphor of trench warfare to illustrate the stages of progress made in his seduction of the Head's secretary, Fiona. He seems keen to share the details of his sex life with Scripps, which the audience may feel is unattractively 'laddish'. Posner reveals his crush on Dakin and confides in Scripps that he can hardly bear to listen to Dakin's words but neither can he turn away. He expresses his pain and longing by singing a verse or two of 'Bewitched, Bothered and Bewildered', and the class returns to the stage.

Hector's lesson contrasts with Irwin's in that it appears to be exhilarating, free-ranging and full of literary references. It is also revealed that he teaches behind a locked door. The boys perform a scene from *Now, Voyager*, a film about a forbidden love affair, in what appears to be a well-established game.

Hector recognises the scene and the boys' money is added to a pot which now contains £16.00. Hector and the boys leave the hard-working Rudge alone on stage.

Mrs Lintott enters and she and Rudge discuss Irwin's methods. Rudge expresses his appreciation of the firm foundations her teaching provided but is also clearly impressed by Irwin, describing his methods as 'cutting-edge' (p. 34).

In another classroom scene, we witness Irwin's lesson and gain further understanding of his unconventional view of history:

Key quotation

Irwin *History nowadays is not a matter of conviction. It's a performance. It's entertainment.' (p. 35)*

Scripps's 'flash-forward' speech refers to Irwin as a 'well-known' historian in the future, who would one day 'notoriously' claim that President Roosevelt was to blame for the attack on **Pearl Harbor**.

Irwin questions the boys on Hector's lessons, poetry and why Hector insists on teaching with the door locked:

Key quotation

Akthar *It's locked against the future, sir. (p. 36)*

Pearl Harbor: the United States naval base in Hawaii which was attacked by the Japanese navy on 7 December 1941. This surprise strike led to the United States' entry into the Second World War

It is apparent that the boys are at this stage still resisting Irwin's methods through their quick-fire, evasive answers, their 'showing off' of their knowledge, the repeated ironic use of the word 'sir' and in some of their questioning about his private life. Irwin is outnumbered and outmanoeuvred. They express or pretend shock that what Hector has taught them could be used in an exam:

Key quotation

Timms *Mr Hector's stuff's not meant for the exam, sir. It's to make us more rounded human beings. (p. 38)*

When Irwin asks them how much more they have up their sleeves, the boys perform an extract from another camp classic about a failed love affair, *Brief Encounter*, which Irwin recognises, but dismisses as a 'waste of time' (p. 41).

Section 5: Irwin and Hector clash (pp. 41–50)

This section begins in the staffroom with Irwin in conversation with Mrs Lintott and involves a flashback to Irwin's conversation with Posner. Posner has confided in Irwin that he thinks he may be homosexual, that he is in love with Dakin and that he is the reason Posner wants to get

Brief Encounter: 1945 British film about a doomed platonic love affair between a couple who are married to other people. It is set mostly in a railway station

Key quotation

Scripps *Posner did not say it, but since he seldom took his eyes off Dakin, he knew that Irwin looked at him occasionally too and wanted him to say so. Basically he just wanted company. (p. 44)*

Friedrich Nietzsche: a nineteenth-century German philosopher

into Cambridge. Irwin tries to get information on Hector from a clearly uncomfortable Posner.

Posner, accompanied by Dakin, sings the last verse of the hymn 'When I Survey the Wondrous Cross' which leads into a scene where Dakin and Scripps discuss Scripps's religious beliefs. Scripps expresses his love for God as 'unrequited' echoing Posner's love for Dakin. As the boys discuss literature, it becomes clear that Dakin is coming round to Irwin's methods. His deep embarrassment over his mispronunciation of the name of philosopher **Nietzsche** in front of Irwin is also perhaps a clue to the beginnings of Dakin's crush on him.

Irwin and Hector are then seen disagreeing on examinations. Hector views them as 'the enemy of education' while Irwin sees exams as 'a fact of life' (p. 48). Irwin wants Hector to persuade the boys that they can use what they learn with Hector in the examination, while the boys seem to think that what they learn with Hector is sacrosanct. Hector is outraged by Irwin's trivialising use of the word 'gobbets' to describe what he has taught them:

Key quotation

Irwin *Education isn't something for when they're old and grey and sitting by the fire. It's for now. The exam is next month.*

Hector *And what happens after the exam? Life goes on. Gobbets! (p. 49)*

The Headmaster is concerned about the boys' progress and expresses his doubts about Hector's lessons. This prepares the audience for Hector's dismissal. Mrs Lintott appears as the Headmaster leaves and expresses her contempt for headmasters in general as 'the chief enemy of culture in any school' (p. 50).

Section 6: Hector in trouble and poetry with Posner (pp. 50–57)

This is a key scene as it heralds Hector's eventual downfall. He is called to see the Headmaster whose wife has witnessed Hector 'fiddling' with a boy on the pillion of his motorbike. The Headmaster pushes Hector to take early retirement and share lessons with Irwin. Hector's words 'Nothing happened' suggest he fails to see the incident as serious while the enraged Headmaster dismisses some famous gay artists and thinkers as 'shrunken violets' (p. 53)

After learning that Dakin is working on past papers with Irwin, a practice Hector refers to as 'Pornography' (p. 53), Hector discusses Hardy's poem 'Drummer Hodge' with Posner. During the discussion, Hector seems to link himself to Hardy, remarking that he had a 'Saddish life, though not unappreciated' (p. 55). A link between the young Posner with his struggle ahead of him and the young drummer is made, both young boys being unprepared for battle, whether actual or metaphorical.

Bennett's stage directions reveal the closeness between Hector and Posner:

Key quotation

He puts out his hand, and it seems for a moment as if Posner will take it, or even that Hector may put it on Posner's knee. But the moment passes. (p. 56)

In contrast with Irwin's earlier heartless dismissal of the 'Unknown Soldier', Hector considers the importance of Hodge having a name, and his sensitivity and love of literature is made clear:

Key quotation

Hector *The best moments in reading are when you come across something — a thought, a feeling, a way of looking at things — which you had thought special and particular to you. (p. 56)*

When Dakin arrives for his 'turn on the bike' Hector refuses and exits, leaving both boys puzzled. Bennett's use of dramatic irony here is clear: the audience, of course, is fully aware of Hector's reasons.

Act Two

- Irwin as celebrity historian meets Posner
- Hector breaks down in despair
- Mrs Lintott reveals her disdain for the Headmaster
- The 'shared lesson' on the Holocaust
- Most of the boys have taken on Irwin's method
- Posner's parents complain about Irwin
- The 'mock' interviews
- Dakin and Irwin discuss history
- The boys depart for Oxbridge
- All are successful
- Dakin arranges a date with Irwin
- The motorbike accident
- Hector's memorial service

Section 1: Irwin as television historian 5 years on (pp. 58–63)

As in Act One, the second Act begins with a flash-forward, this time of about 5 years. Irwin, wheelchair bound, is now a television historian filming at Rievaulx Abbey, Yorkshire and struggling with his lines. Thus it is apparent that whatever happened to Irwin occurred much closer to the action of the play than we might previously have thought. Irwin's 'angle' is clear, and we hear him repeating the lines about Henry VIII that he used with the boys in Act One.

Between takes he is approached by a man who clearly knows his background.

The man turns out to be Posner who seems to have had some kind of breakdown, having dropped out of Cambridge. This casts a shadow over the second Act, since the young Posner is a sympathetic character. Calling his character 'Man' also indicates the passage of time: Posner is no longer a boy. He is trying to get a story on the now famous Irwin, with particular reference to his 'relationship' with Dakin.

Irwin's utter cynicism and belief in style over substance is confirmed by his comment on his use of a wheelchair, which he sees as helpful to his image:

Key quotation

Irwin *Disability brings with it an assumption of sincerity. (p. 60)*

Section 2: Hector breaks down and the truth is revealed (pages 63–69)

This is the first lesson with the boys since Hector's interview with the Head. Bennett builds sympathy for him by showing both his vulnerability and his true feelings about his situation. Hector, in a 'sombre and distracted mood' (p. 63), and unable to indulge in the usual banter, he breaks down in front of the boys in grief and self-disgust:

Key quotation

Hector *What made me piss my life away in this god-forsaken place? There's nothing of me left. (p. 65)*

Posner is the only one of the embarrassed boys who goes to him and 'pats Hector rather awkwardly on the back' (p. 65). In an attempt to cheer Hector up, the film game is played and Hector wins by recognising *The Seventh Veil*.

The Headmaster reveals to Mrs Lintott the details of Hector's indiscretion, pleased that he now has an excuse to get rid of him, principally because his results are 'unpredictable and unquantifiable' (p. 67).

After the Headmaster leaves, Mrs Lintott addresses the audience directly, revealing her contempt for the Headmaster's views. Her statement that she has not, until now, been allotted 'an inner voice' (p. 68) is an ironic recognition of the all-male world of the play.

The Seventh Veil: 1945 melodrama about the life of an acclaimed but psychologically damaged classical pianist

GRADE *BOOSTER*

Always take note of what happens and when. Bennett will often follow a darker moment with a moment of light relief in order to break the tension.

Section 3: A shared lesson, the Holocaust, and a letter of complaint (pp. 70–81)

The first shared lesson between Irwin and Hector enables the audience to see the contrast in their approaches, a contrast brought out by Timms:

Key quotation

Timms *It depends if you want us thoughtful. Or smart. (p. 70)*

The gulf between them is further emphasised by the discussion on the Holocaust which follows. Posner (who is Jewish) and Hector see the horror, whereas Irwin encourages them to 'Distance yourselves' (p. 74). Irwin's willingness to encourage the boys to take an event so dark and so dreadful and to use it for their own ends suggests that nothing is sacred to such a person.

Hector is increasingly dismayed at the way the boys are adapting to Irwin's approach as is shown by their respective reactions to the lesson.

After the lesson Dakin flirts with Irwin, unable to understand why he feels such a strong compulsion to please him.

Dakin then reveals to Scripps that he knows the real reason Hector is leaving. As they discuss Hector's fumbling on the bike, it is clear that they do not take it seriously:

Key quotation

Dakin *Are we scarred for life, do you think?*

Scripps *We must hope so. Perhaps it will turn me into* **Proust**. *(p. 77)*

The scene shifts to the Headmaster's study. The Headmaster has received a complaint from Posner's parents concerning Irwin's comments on the Holocaust. The Headmaster sees Mr Posner as 'a little overexcited' but his main concern is that Posner's father might complain to the school governors and Irwin is told to write a letter of apology.

Irwin and Posner discuss using the Holocaust in an examination, with Irwin first accepting responsibility for Posner's trouble with his family, but still cynically advising him to 'surprise' the examiners:

Key quotation

Irwin *You're Jewish. You can get away with a lot more than the other candidates. (p. 80)*

Marcel Proust: a highly acclaimed French novelist. His greatest novel *In Search of Lost Time* (*À la Recherche du Temps Perdu*) deals with the power of memory

Build critical skills

Dakin tells Irwin that the boys have been discussing whether Irwin is 'disingenuous' or 'meretricious' (p. 75). At this stage in the play, which of these words do you think best describes Irwin?

Dakin is developing a 'crush' on Irwin, even beginning to write like him. Posner reveals that Irwin also likes Dakin in return as he has noticed that Irwin 'seldom looks at anyone else' (p. 81).

Section 4: Preparing for Oxbridge (pp. 82–96)

Hector, Irwin and Mrs Lintott conduct mock interviews to prepare the boys for their Oxbridge experience. Irwin believes that the boys should not admit to liking anything which 'everyone likes' and advises them to claim knowledge 'more off the beaten track'. Hector believes that they should simply 'tell the truth' (p. 83).

Mrs Lintott is annoyed by the assumption that the interviewing dons will all be men and takes the opportunity to offer a woman's view of history:

Key quotation

Mrs Lintott *History is a commentary on the various and continuing incapabilities of men. What is history? History is women following behind with the bucket. (p. 85)*

In a 'pausy conversation, with Dakin more master than pupil' (p. 88) and heavy with sexual undertones, Irwin and Dakin discuss 'make[ing] moves' and the random nature of history.

A photograph is taken before the boys leave for their interviews, during which the Headmaster's crassness is illustrated once more when he belittles Posner and excludes Hector. The boys leave to the tune of 'Wish Me Luck as You Wave Me Goodbye'.

The exchange between Mrs Lintott and Irwin on Hector's being spotted by 'Mrs Headmaster' suggests she has some sympathy for his misfortune. It also further emphasises the randomness of history, while preparing the audience for Hector's accident.

Hector and Irwin discuss boys and Hector tells him that he is no longer moved by them as they have become work, finishing the conversation with a warning to Irwin:

Key quotation

Hector *Don't touch him. He'll think you're a fool. That's what they think about me. (p. 95)*

Even at this stage, Hector tries to underplay the incident on the motorbike to Mrs Lintott, referring to it as 'more in benediction than gratification' (p. 95), a claim which she dismisses:

Mrs Lintott *A grope is a grope.* (p. 95)

Scripps, Dakin, and Posner each describe their time at the interviews in a short monologue. Scripps visited the college chapel, Dakin describes the student's room he stayed in, and Posner 'sat in the room most of the time or trailed around the streets' (p. 96) emphasising the sense of him as an outsider and foreshadowing his later problems.

Section 5: Success and tragedy (pp. 97–109)

The boys 'erupt' onto the stage, which suggests their great excitement, and the Headmaster congratulates Irwin on the boys' success, adding thanks to Mrs Lintott as an afterthought. We learn that Posner has gained a 'scholarship', Dakin has an 'exhibition', and all the other boys have 'places'. Although at this stage it is wrongly assumed that Rudge has been unsuccessful, we soon learn that he has gained a place thanks to 'family connections' (p. 97), his father having been a college servant.

Dakin tells Irwin that he knows he did not attend Corpus and Irwin admits to the lie, revealing that he actually attended Bristol University and only went to Oxford to 'do a teaching diploma' (p. 99).

Dakin invites Irwin to go for a drink. This is swiftly followed by a more explicit invitation concerning a sexual act. Under pressure from Dakin, who mocks Irwin's reluctance to take action, Irwin agrees and an arrangement is made for the following Sunday afternoon.

Dakin tells Scripps that his offer to Irwin was because he 'just wanted to say thank you' (p. 102) and reveals that he has blackmailed the Headmaster to keep Hector on by using his knowledge of the Headmaster's attempts to touch Fiona inappropriately. He then 'rewards' Posner with a brief embrace and puts on the motorcycle helmet to also 'reward' Hector.

In the final game, Rudge sings 'It's a Sin' by the Pet Shop Boys despite the disapproval of Timms, and Hector awards him the jackpot.

The Headmaster enters and forbids Hector to take a boy on his motorbike, suggesting instead that Irwin should accompany Hector. Scripps as narrator highlights the moment as one where 'history rattled over the points' (p. 105).

Scripps now relates the details of the crash which has resulted in Hector's death and Irwin being confined to a wheelchair. One theory surrounding the accident is particularly ironic, as Scripps says: 'Trust Irwin to lean the opposite way to everyone else' (p. 105).

Build critical skills

Why is Scripps's comment, 'Trust Irwin to lean the opposite way to everyone else' (p. 105) ironic? What is its effect here?

Irwin remembers nothing of the accident and we learn that the assignation with Dakin never takes place, as Dakin rather shallowly admits, 'I couldn't face the wheelchair' (p. 106).

The final pages of the play take place in double time as Bennett blends Hector's memorial service with Mrs Lintott bringing the audience up to date with what has happened to the boys in the years after the events of the play.

The Headmaster's words about Hector are clichéd and hypocritical, but the boys' comments are moving and sincere:

Key quotations

Lockwood *It was the first time I realised a teacher was a human being.* (p. 106)

Crowther *He was stained and shabby and did unforgivable things but he led you to expect the best.* (p. 107)

Scripps *Love apart, it is the only education worth having.* (p. 109)

Build critical skills

Hector *Finish, good lady, the bright day is done and we are for the dark.* (p. 108)

This line is a quotation from Act V scene 2 of Shakespeare's play *Antony and Cleopatra*. In what ways do you think it is appropriate here?

The audience learns that Crowther and Lockwood became magistrates, Akthar a headmaster, Timms an owner of a chain of dry cleaners, and Dakin a 'tax lawyer, telling highly paid fibs' (p. 107). Rudge is in the building trade and Scripps is a journalist on a 'better class of paper' (p. 108).

Only Posner we are told 'truly took everything to heart' and lives alone, suffering 'periodic breakdowns' (p. 108).

The play ends with the words of Hector, explaining his attitude to education and the importance of knowledge:

Key quotation

Hector *Pass the parcel. That's sometimes all you can do. Take it, feel it and pass it on. Not for me, not for you, but for someone, somewhere, one day.* (p. 109)

GRADE BOOSTER

Turn to the Top ten section for ten short, memorable quotations on key moments in the play. You will also find this useful as a brief summary of the plot.

GRADE *FOCUS*

Grade 5

To achieve Grade 5, students must show a clear and detailed understanding of the whole text and of the effects created by its structure.

Grade 8

To achieve Grade 8, students' responses will display a comprehensive understanding of explicit and implicit meanings in the text as a whole and will examine and evaluate the writer's use of structure in detail.

REVIEW YOUR LEARNING

1. Why does the Headmaster decide to bring in Irwin to teach the boys?
2. What setting do the boys choose for the French lesson?
3. What song does Posner sing to express his feelings for Dakin?
4. What reasons do the boys give for Hector's classroom door being locked?
5. Posner confides in Irwin. What does he tell him?
6. Who spots Hector 'fiddling' with a boy on his motorbike?
7. How does Bennett indicate a moment of closeness between Hector and Posner during the tutorial?
8. Why does Irwin go on the back of the motorbike instead of Dakin?
9. What happens to Irwin and Hector as a result?
10. What does Mrs Lintott tell us about the eventual fate of Posner?

Answers on p. 102.

Target your thinking

- Who are the key characters in the play? (**AO1**)
- How does Bennett create believable characters within the context of the play? (**AO2**)
- What purposes are served by the characters? (**AO1, AO2**)

Bennett presents the characters in *The History Boys* through a combination of techniques:

- What the characters say.
- What the characters do.
- What other characters say to them and about them.
- Through stage directions, music and projected images.

Hector

Named after a Greek hero, Hector is a charismatic figure, described by Bennett on his first entrance as a 'man of studied eccentricity' (p. 4) which perhaps suggests a hint of performance in his make-up. Refusing to conform to modern teaching styles, he teaches behind a locked door, and strongly objects to the Headmaster's determination to achieve Oxbridge places for the boys by any means necessary.

The audience would probably feel that Hector represents an old style of teaching, and through his role in the play Bennett is perhaps inviting us to consider what makes a good teacher by contrasting his classroom style with the more cynical approach of Irwin.

Hector's touching of the boys who ride pillion on his motorbike is clearly morally wrong, not to mention dangerous, and his failure to face up to the truth about his actions is extremely troubling, especially to a modern audience. However, it is also true that he inspires his students, making learning both engaging and fun, as we witness in the bawdy French lesson in Act One, as well as in the 'film games' he enacts with the boys. Furthermore, even though his approaches to education seem likely to be overtaken by Irwin's, it becomes clear at his 'memorial service' that he is remembered with fondness by the boys he has taught, even if they remain unsure of his intentions.

◀ Hector in the classroom in the 2006 film version of the play

Key quotation

Akthar *There was a contract between him and his class. Quite what the contract was or what it involved would be hard to say. But it was there. (p. 106)*

In sharp contrast to Irwin, whose approach he views as mere 'journalism', Hector is presented as having no interest in exams; his teaching is concerned with the pursuit of knowledge for its own sake.

Hector has a genuine love of literature, as is movingly revealed in his discussion of Hardy's poem 'Drummer Hodge' with Posner, and he, somewhat unfashionably, encourages the boys to learn poetry by heart. However, he feels strongly that this knowledge is to enrich the boys' future, and objects to it being used to help them pass exams, which he views as 'the enemy of education' (p. 48).

In spite of Hector's 'weaknesses', it is clear that Bennett expects the audience to sympathise with him at least to some degree; the final lines of the play belong to Hector and his views on education:

Key quotation

Pass it on, boys.

That's the game I wanted you to learn.

Pass it on. (p. 109)

Irwin

It is Irwin who opens the play in the role of a government advisor or 'spin doctor' in his forties who is giving MPs rather cynical advice on how they might deal with putting a positive spin on an unpopular bill. Irwin suggests that 'Paradox works well...' (p. 1) and this thought leads him back to thinking about school and his experience as a teacher.

Bennett also uses Irwin to open the second Act where we see him in the role of a television historian. These two glimpses into Irwin's later life suggest that Bennett perhaps sees the likes of Irwin as representing the future of education, the media and politics.

Irwin seems to represent what Nick Hytner, the original director of the play, referred to as 'swashbuckling **relativism**' in a *Guardian* interview, 17 October 2006.

relativism: a school of thought which suggests there is no absolute truth or morality. All points of view are equally valid

Irwin is clearly bright. Bennett signals this fact during the French lesson when he uses the unusual word, '*commotionné*' meaning shell-shocked. This appears to stop the boys in their tracks as the stage directions tell us: '*The classroom falls silent at this unexpected intrusion.*' Even Hector appears nonplussed: 'Comment?' When Irwin defines the word, Bennett again uses stage directions to tell us that, '*There is a perceptible moment*' (p. 16). This interruption is important as it is an indication of Irwin's dramatic role as an intruder into the cosy world of the school and the instigator of change.

Irwin appears to have no regard for the truth, having misled the school and students about having gained his degree at Oxford. His mission is to

Irwin and Mrs Lintott in ▶ the 2006 film version of the play teach the boys a flashy 'trick' to help them gain Oxbridge success. This consists of taking any accepted view of an historical event or person, and, regardless of what you may yourself believe, gain attention by arguing the opposite. This approach backfires on him when Posner's parents object to his 'angle' on the Holocaust and he is forced to write a letter of apology. However, in his favour, it might be said that his approach does appear to work and enables boys from state school backgrounds to gain places at Oxbridge.

Although Irwin is shown as brash and cynical in his approach to education, Bennett presents him as a private man who is unwilling to reveal any details of his personal life or to admit his true feelings towards Dakin. He appears weak in that towards the end he agrees to meet with Dakin, against his better judgement. He offers little help to the troubled Posner, when he confides in him, seeming more concerned with protecting himself. To begin with, the boys seem to have the upper hand with him, mocking what they see as his attempt to curry favour by making reference to foreskins and masturbation. However, the boys come around to him as they begin to see that his teaching may have a practical use. Clearly, the boys he teaches achieve great success in that every single one of them is accepted for Oxbridge.

GRADE *BOOSTER*

Remember that you too can improve your grade by offering alternative interpretations, a bit like Irwin does! Just always bear in mind that these interpretations must always be supported by evidence from the text.

Irwin is, of course, presented in direct contrast to Hector, something which Bennett makes clear in their exchange after the 'shared lesson', the success of which they see in very different terms, Irwin being 'encouraged' and Hector dismissing the boys as 'parrots' (p. 75).

Build critical skills

At the end of the play, Irwin says of Hector 'He was a good man but I do not think there is time for his kind of teaching any more' (p. 108).

What does this suggest to you about the future of education? Is it all about jumping through hoops to gain rewards, or is education important for its own sake, for example?

Key quotation

Irwin *...truth is no more at issue in an examination than thirst at a wine-tasting or fashion at a striptease.* (p. 26)

Build critical skills

How do you respond to Irwin as a teacher? Can you reconcile the fact that he is successful in helping all the boys to get into Oxbridge with his fundamental lack of honesty? Do we expect higher standards of behaviour from teachers than we would from people in other professions?

Mrs Lintott

Build critical skills

Mrs Lintott describes her role as one of 'patient and not unamused sufferance of the predilections and preoccupations of men. They kick their particular stone along the street and I watch' (p. 68).

How does this enhance your understanding of Bennett's presentation of her?

As the only female character on stage, Mrs Lintott offers a different perspective on the patriarchal assumptions and vanities of the male society of the boys' school. With her 'size seven court shoe[s], broad fitting' (p. 96), she appears to represent solid common sense while exposing the foolishness and arrogance of the men. She is a sympathetic character, and her role as confidante to Hector and Irwin allows the audience to gain some further understanding of both.

She is presented by Bennett as a competent and respected teacher. Rudge reveals that he values her input as 'firm foundations' (p. 33). Her view that 'Plainly stated and properly organised facts need no presentation...' (p. 8) sums up her approach to education.

However, she largely conforms to her own analysis of the feminine approach, 'rueful, accepting, taking things as you find them' (p. 84), such as when she accepts that Irwin will take over the teaching of her boys.

She is told that while she has done an admirable job in getting good A-level results for the boys, someone else will be brought in to improve 'presentation'. Though she mocks the pretensions of the Headmaster with her incisive comment 'A sprig of parsley do you mean? Or an umbrella in the cocktail?' when he says 'Think charm. Think polish. Think Renaissance Man' her actual answer is 'Yes, Headmaster' (p. 9).

She appears detached from the chaos of sexual desire, since it is implied by Bennett that her first pizza in Durham was more memorable than her first sexual encounter. Bennett presents her as a character who shows no sexual desire, in comparison with the three male adults and most of the boys, who seem to exist in a blizzard of hormones. This, of course, may reflect Bennett's perception of middle-aged women as somewhat asexual creatures. She, on the other hand, is clear-sighted and perceptive. For example, she recognises that Dakin is obsessed with sex rather than 'sad', and that Hector's defence of his groping as a 'benediction' is 'the most colossal balls' (p. 95).

Bennett allows her an inner voice in which she reveals her contempt for the Headmaster but she never speaks of it directly to him (p. 68). Her use of taboo language in doing so is perhaps a little unexpected in terms of stereotypical ideas about middle-aged, middle-class women. The audience laugh, but they may also be encouraged to think a little more carefully and wonder whether her calm exterior conceals a deeper anger.

This comes closest to expression in her dismay that, despite having taught the boys history on 'a non-gender orientated basis' (p. 83), it does not appear to have occurred to any of the boys that one of the interviewing dons might be a woman. In addition, she states that history is 'a commentary on the various and continuing incapabilities of men', while recognising that all of the men present in this scene find her 'undisguised expression of feeling distasteful' (p. 85).

Finally, it is the trusted voice of Mrs Lintott that Bennett uses in the moving last scene where she reveals the different fates of the various boys.

Key quotation

Mrs Lintott *What is history? History is women following behind with the bucket.* (p. 85)

GRADE BOOSTER

```
Always remember that the characters in the play have
been created by a writer and that your focus needs to
be on the ways that the writer has made the characters
come alive for the reader. Don't write about the
characters as if they were real people. If the words
'Bennett' or 'the writer' do not appear several times
in your answer you are probably not answering the
question and you are unlikely to achieve high marks.
```

The Headmaster

Bennett's presentation of the Headmaster is an unsympathetic one. Almost the first thing we learn about him is his desire for success is in terms of league tables and that his educational values are based on snobbery and self-promotion. Ironically, he criticises the boys for being 'a little...ordinaire' (p. 9) while stumbling over his own participation in the French lesson and failing to understand what is actually going on. This, together with Mrs Lintott's mockery of him, presents him as a fool from the beginning of the play.

As Mrs Lintott tells Irwin, 'the chief enemy of culture in any school is always the Headmaster' (p. 50).

The Headmaster wants the students to have 'polish' rather than a real education, and advises Irwin, not on teaching methods, but to grow a moustache to help with his classroom control! When Posner's parents object to Irwin's teaching of the Holocaust, his concern is more to do with the fact that they will complain to the governors, rather than the nature of the teaching or Irwin's insensitivity. In this way, Bennett leads the audience towards the realisation that this is a man who is concerned mainly with appearances.

He is happy to have evidence of Hector's misconduct because it gives him an excuse to get rid of a teacher whose results are 'unpredictable and unquantifiable' (p. 67). His objections are not based on possible damage to the boys, just on the idea that, 'This is a school and it isn't normal' (p. 53).

He is also a hypocrite in that his sexual harassment of his secretary parallels Hector's actions towards the boys. He reverses his decision as a result of implied blackmail from Dakin, again revealing himself as motivated by self-interest rather than morality.

His lack of genuine feeling is evidenced in the trite eulogy he gives at Hector's funeral.

Dakin

Dakin is presented by Bennett as perhaps the most confident of the boys; he is described by Hector as 'a good-looking boy' (p. 22) and by Mrs Lintott in more vulgar terms. Dakin's intelligence is revealed by his understanding of the 'game' (p. 20) which Irwin is teaching them to play with history, as a way of gaining a university place, and Irwin also recognises him as 'the canniest' (p. 50) of the group.

Apart from Rudge, Dakin is the only one of the boys having sex, and he is presented often bragging about his relationship with Fiona, the Headmaster's secretary. Dakin describes this using an extended metaphor of warfare, suggesting he has no real feelings for Fiona, seeing her simply as someone to be conquered. Some audience members will see this as amusing, but others may be repelled by this unattractive sexism.

Dakin uses the possibility of sex to get what he wants, manipulating both Hector and Irwin in this way. He offers himself to Irwin as a reward or a thank you for helping him get his scholarship to Oxford, but he also appears to have a crush on Irwin, as evidenced by his horror at mispronouncing Nietzsche in his presence.

Dakin is used by Bennett to drive key events in the story, for example ensuring that Hector is reinstated at the school by blackmailing the Headmaster about his behaviour towards Fiona. He also discovers that Irwin has lied about his claim to have attended Oxford University, a point on which audiences may judge Irwin.

By the end of the play, Dakin is revealed to be a somewhat shallow person who cares little about other people. He has always known that Posner has feelings for him, and 'Posner's reward' (p. 103) is no more than the briefest of hugs. Equally, he is happy to admit, rather offensively, he does not follow up the relationship with Irwin as he 'couldn't face the wheelchair' (p. 106).

His eventual career as a 'highly paid' tax lawyer (p. 107), or at least Mrs Lintott's reaction to it, also suggests he is both dishonest and driven by financial gain.

Posner

Posner is presented initially as the 'dictionary person' (p. 63) a role that gives him a purpose, and expresses the idea that he is anxious to learn. He is also used as a device to explain the meaning of words with which the audience might be unfamiliar. For example, in the first classroom scene, when Hector uses the term 'euphemism' to describe the Headmaster's description of his lessons as general studies, Posner reads out loud from the dictionary. '"Euphemism...substitution of mild or vague or roundabout expression for a harsh or direct one"' (p. 5).

As well as that, he sings many of the songs including the hauntingly beautiful 'Bewitched, Bothered and Bewildered', and thus much of the emotional power of the play rests within him.

He defines himself as an outsider. Although Bennett presents him with great compassion, there is a sense that he may be doomed from the start, and that he is clearly aware of it.

Although this seems comic at the time, it foreshadows his failure to complete his course at Cambridge and his eventual unhappy and reclusive existence. This idea is supported in the discussion with Hector of the poem 'Drummer Hodge'. In Hector's remarking that the ages of the dead Hodge and Hardy correspond to those of Posner and himself, the effect is that the future of Posner is conjoined in the minds of the audience with that of poor Hodge, another 'lost boy' (p. 55).

He is clearly lacking in self-confidence but is also perceptive enough to realise that within the context of the 1980s, life was not always easy for those from minority groups.

Posner lives with rejection. He is open about his unrequited love for Dakin and confides in Irwin, who he believes shares his passion, that the reason he wants to go to Cambridge is to impress Dakin, a fact that makes him seem both hopeless and naive. Scripps refers to his 'spaniel heart' (p. 81) suggesting his adoring fidelity and perhaps recalling Helena's words to Demetrius in *A Midsummer Night's Dream* (Act 2, scene 1, lines 204–06):

> Use me but as your spaniel, spurn me, strike me,
> Neglect me, lose me; only give me leave,
> Unworthy as I am, to follow you.

However, just as he enjoys playing Celia Johnson in the scene from *Brief Encounter*, (a film with a strong gay sub-text, in that it deals with forbidden love) there is a hint in Posner's self-mockery that he enjoys the drama of suffering:

Key quotation

Posner *Yes, it's only a phase.*

Who says I want it to pass?

But the pain. The pain. (p. 81)

We learn that he would be happy to ride pillion with Hector but that he does not 'fit the bill' (p. 17), perhaps because he is not to Hector's taste.

Key quotation

Posner *I'm a Jew.*

I'm small.

I'm homosexual. And I live in Sheffield.

I'm fucked. (p. 42)

Build critical skills

Posner *I sat in the room most of the time or trailed around the streets. I can see why they make a fuss about it. Every college is like a stately home; my parents would love it. There was a question on the Holocaust. And I did play it down. (p. 96)*

How do Posner's words foreshadow his eventual unhappiness?

He is in many ways presented as the most sensitive and empathetic of the boys, in that it is he who attempts to comfort a despairing Hector by rubbing his back. This is highlighted by Bennett in the stage directions:

Key quotation

Scripps is nearest to him and ought to touch him, but doesn't, nor does Dakin.

Posner is the one who comes and after some hesitation pats Hector rather awkwardly on the back... *(p. 65)*

He initially questions Irwin's approach to the Holocaust but betrays his heritage in order to win a scholarship to Cambridge:

Key quotation

Posner *There was a question on the Holocaust. And I did play it down. (p. 96)*

At the end of the play he is singled out by Mrs Lintott:

Key quotation

Mrs Lintott *Still, of all Hector's boys, there is only one who truly took everything to heart, remembers everything he was ever taught...the songs, the poems, the sayings, the endings; the words of Hector never forgotten. (p. 108)*

but since he has periodic breakdowns and his only friends are on the internet, his fate is ultimately a depressing one.

Scripps

Scripps is presented as a boy for whom religion is important. Bennett also uses him from time to time to play the role of narrator in the play, stepping out from the action to address the audience directly. For example, it is through Scripps that the audience learns about Irwin's later notoriety as a celebrated 'historian' (p. 35). Furthermore, both Dakin and Posner confide in Scripps at key moments in the play, enabling the audience to learn more about Dakin's affair with Fiona and Posner's infatuation with Dakin.

Scripps does not often take a prominent part in the action but he does stand up against Irwin's views on the Holocaust, accusing him of viewing it as 'just another topic on which we may get a question' (p. 74), and he is the last of the boys to speak in the play, offering a sympathetic view of Hector's teaching:

Key quotation

Scripps *Love apart, it is the only education worth having. (p. 109)*

As Scripps's main role is to observe and report, perhaps this suits his eventual career as a journalist 'on a better class of paper' (p. 108).

Rudge

Rudge is presented as a hard-working student who is the least academic of the boys, but nevertheless is determined to get into Christ Church College, Oxford. In the mock interviews he explains that he believes it is the one that he might be able to get into. The Headmaster dismissively regards him as an 'oddity' and as having 'No hope' of achieving a place at 'Christ Church of all places' (p. 11), a feat which Rudge actually achieves, thanks partly to his 'family connections' (p. 97).

His hard-working nature is the key to his success as in later life he becomes a self-made man in the building industry, a career of which he is proud:

Key quotation

Rudge *Like them or not, Rudge Homes are at least affordable homes for first-time buyers. (p. 107)*

He excels at sports and points out that playing golf can be more of an asset to achieving success than all the brains of the other boys. Rudge is aware that he is often patronised by the boys and by the teachers, particularly Irwin, who criticises him for relying on the teacher's words, rather than thinking for himself:

Key quotation

Irwin *You can write down, Rudge, that 'I must not write down every word that teacher says.' (p. 26)*

Rudge's down-to-earth approach to life and learning is admirable and is perhaps reflected in the sound of his name, a name which perhaps also links him with the name of Hodge. He is also, in his definition of history and his attitude to sex, often amusing.

Build critical skills

Reread the section where Rudge is interviewed by the teachers prior to his trip to Oxbridge. How has Bennett made this passage of the play both amusing and revealing?

Timms

Bennett presents Timms as a kind of class clown as he is the one who makes a cheeky comment in the conversation with Mrs Lintott about the lack of women historians. It is he who claims not to understand poetry and he plays the Bette Davis role in the enactment of the scene from *Now, Voyager*, as well as Claudine in the French brothel scene. In later life, he 'puts together a chain of dry cleaners and takes drugs at the weekend' (p. 107), suggesting a somewhat mundane life punctuated by short-term, self-indulgent pleasure seeking.

Lockwood, Akthar and Crowther

The last three boys are not given particularly strong characteristics. They take part in the repartee with both Hector and Irwin and end up as 'pillars of a community that no longer has much use for pillars' (p. 107), Akthar as a headmaster and the other two as magistrates.

GRADE BOOSTER

```
Turn to the Top ten section for short memorable
quotations on the main characters. You will find it
very useful to have them at your fingertips in the
examination.
```

GRADE FOCUS

Grade 5

To achieve Grade 5, students will develop a clear understanding of how Bennett uses language, form and structure to create characters, supported by appropriate references to the text.

Grade 8

To achieve Grade 8, students will examine and evaluate the ways that Bennett uses language, form and structure to create characters, supported by carefully chosen and well-integrated references to the text.

REVIEW YOUR LEARNING

1 What is the significance of the name Hector?

2 What is Hector's view of examinations?

3 What do you understand by the term 'relativism', and how does it apply to Irwin?

4 How might you sum up Mrs Lintott's attitude to education?

5 How does Bennett present the Headmaster as a hypocrite in the play?

6 What is Dakin's eventual job?

7 What evidence is there to suggest Dakin's shallow nature?

8 Why does Posner wish to go to Cambridge?

9 What does Scripps do that helps the audience see him as a kind of narrator in the play?

10 How is Rudge described by the Headmaster?

Answers on p. 103.

Target your thinking

- What is a theme? (**AO1, AO3**)
- What are the main themes in *The History Boys*? (**AO1, AO3**)
- What is a motif? (**AO1, AO3**)
- What is the main motif that occurs in *The History Boys*? (**AO1, AO3**)

In literature, a theme is an idea that a writer explores through language, form and structure. A theme raises questions in the minds of readers or audience members. It is something that the writer wants you to think about. It might appear in an examination question as 'ideas about…' Sometimes, writers just want you to explore what you think about a particular theme. They may pose questions rather than offering answers. However, in some instances, writers may hope that as a result of thinking about a particular theme, readers may change their attitudes and even their behaviour.

> **GRADE** *BOOSTER*
>
> In writing about themes in the examination, you need to be aware of the questions that are being asked, and you need to show that you have thought about them deeply. You do not need to come up with definitive answers.

There are several different ways of categorising themes, and in any interpretation of literary themes, there is bound to be some overlap. The main themes of *The History Boys* might be grouped as follows:

- education
- history
- sex and sexuality

Education

At the heart of the play is Bennett's exploration of the purposes and nature of education.

The Headmaster cares only for the outward trappings of success. He is unable to see past the idea of rising up the league tables. He is less concerned with the boys themselves than with the reputation of the

A. E. Housman: English poet (1859–1936) who was inspired mainly by the countryside

school. He wants his school to equal well-known public schools, such as 'Manchester Grammar School, Haberdashers' Aske's' (p. 11). He wants the boys to acquire 'charm' and 'polish' which he sees as the key to Oxbridge success and Irwin is brought in to achieve this.

Mrs Lintott, the only female teacher, represents an approach which foregrounds the importance of 'properly organised facts' (p. 9). It is she who is responsible for the very good A-level results the boys achieved.

However, it is Irwin and Hector who are used by Bennett to present two polar opposites in educational philosophy. Hector, for instance, represents a passionate love of learning for its own sake: he takes **A. E. Housman's** view that 'All knowledge is precious whether or not it serves the slightest human use' (p. 5).

Mrs Lintott tells us: 'Hector never bothered with what he was educating these boys for' (p. 107). Unconventional and charismatic, he inspires his boys with his unorthodox approach and nourishes them with a combination of poetry, general knowledge and joyful silliness.

When Timms states that he doesn't always understand poetry, Hector cheerily replies that he never understands it but that they should learn it now and understand it later, when it will be an antidote to their various life experiences. Put simply, for Hector, education is for life. He congratulates the boys on their A-level results, but refers to them somewhat disparagingly as 'those longed-for emblems of conformity' (p. 4) and refers to a CV as a 'Cheat's Visa' (p. 5).

Even the Headmaster can see that Hector is a good teacher, but he fails to value his teaching because the results are 'unquantifiable' and therefore of no use in assisting the school to ascend the league tables and enhance their reputation. Bennett shows the audience just how effective he is as a teacher when he gently leads Posner in a discussion of the Thomas Hardy poem 'Drummer Hodge'. Both the man and the boy are, like Hodge, 'Un-kissed. Un-rejoicing. Un-confessed. Un-embraced' (p. 55) and this creates greater understanding and compassion for them both. Cleverly, Bennett also uses this scene to demonstrate the great power of literature to reach out across the years so that 'it is as if a hand has come out and taken yours' (p. 56). This functions as a validation of Hector's views on poetry.

For Irwin, though, literature and history are there to be used for one's own ends, in this case to impress the dons, pass the entrance exam and gain places at Oxbridge. He teaches the boys how to play the system. Therefore, it is not a case of 'Speak what we feel, not what we ought to say' (p. 7) as Posner says when quoting *King Lear* in Act One. The approach that Irwin recommends is to take an accepted view and then argue the opposite, regardless of what you yourself might feel about it:

Build critical skills

Hector believes that examinations are 'the enemy of education'. Do you agree?

Build critical skills

Read again the important scene where Hector and Posner discuss the poem 'Drummer Hodge'. How has Bennett made the scene so moving for the audience?

Key quotation

Irwin *...take* **Stalin***. Generally agreed to be a monster, and rightly. So dissent. Find something, anything, to say in his defence. (p. 35)*

He urges the boys to use aspects of what he refers to as 'the gobbets' they have learnt in Hector's lessons, such as the ability to quote the poetry of Auden. Although they initially feign shock, they do come to see the usefulness of this approach, and as they are all accepted by Oxbridge, it is clearly successful in terms of what Irwin sets out to do.

The difference between the two approaches is shown most clearly in the shared lesson on the Holocaust. Posner and Scripps are clearly irritated by Irwin:

Key quotation

Irwin *Good point.*

Scripps *You keep saying, 'Good point.' Not good point, sir. True. (p. 74)*

However, Lockwood demonstrates that he has grasped the Irwin method:

Key quotation

Hector *Why can you not simply condemn the camps outright as an unprecedented horror?*

There is slight embarrassment.

Lockwood *No point, sir. Everybody will do that. That's the stock answer, sir... the camps an event unlike any other, the evil unprecedented, etc., etc. (p. 73)*

Joseph Stalin: leader of the Soviet Union from the mid-1920s to his death in 1953. Regarded by most as an extremely cruel dictator

◄ Auschwitz concentration camp

Most of the audience will share Hector's shock at the use of 'etcetera', in which the dead are 'reduced to a mere verbal abbreviation' (p. 73). They may also have some sympathy with Hector's stance in the mock interviews when the students are asked about their interests: 'Why can they not just all tell the truth?' (p. 83).

Therefore, in the context of Hector's death and funeral, it seems as if the weight of the argument is with Hector. The boys' moving tributes suggest that they do value what they learnt from Hector, especially since Scripps's words are positioned so close to the end of the play:

Key quotation

Scripps *Love apart, it is the only education worth having. (p. 109)*

Hector himself has the very last words in his exhortation to 'Pass it on' (p. 109).

However, to see the play as simply a condemnation of Irwin's methods and a ringing endorsement of Hector's is to perhaps oversimplify the argument. Nick Hytner, director of the original production, states:

> 'The truth is that much of what Hector teaches is entirely self-indulgent. … and his insistence on inflicting on his class the culture, high and low, of his own youth, is at least questionable.' (*Guardian*, 15 September 2006)

He also recognises that what most parents would prefer is Irwin's approach, as Irwin does offer these young people from ordinary backgrounds a way to access what is commonly regarded as the pinnacle of higher education in this country.

If you have ever experienced the cutting short of a fascinating and undoubtedly worthwhile discussion because it is not relevant to your preparation for an exam you so desperately want to pass, you will be familiar with this issue. It may be that as teachers and students who study the play, we need to recognise our own conflicting attitudes. We may desire education for its own sake and see it as an absolute ideal, yet also feel that we are bound by the restrictions of life in the real world, where most of us believe that it is examination success which is the key to opportunity and progression. Clearly, there are no easy answers.

GRADE **BOOSTER**

Examination questions may ask you to consider how Bennett uses a particular character or characters to present a theme. For example, how does Bennett present ideas about education through the characters of Irwin and/or Hector? Learn to think of characters in this way.

History

Within the play, the nature of history is one of the central ideas that is explored. The play itself takes place in the past, as the opening scene with Irwin and the MPs suggests that Irwin is in his forties. The stage directions tell us that when he arrives at the school, he is about 25. The boys' adult lives, which are revealed in the final moments of the play, can be traced back to their experiences of school.

The theme of history is highlighted initially by the title and by the boys' topic of study. They have all done well in their A-levels having been taught history by Mrs Lintott.

Irwin takes a different view. For him, history is a means to an end. It can be manipulated, cheapened and even lied about as he himself demonstrates by rewriting his own history when he lies about his university background.

In terms of the boys and their ambitions, he recommends taking a generally accepted truth and turning it on its head:

Key quotation

Irwin *The wrong end of the stick is the right one. A question has a front door and a back door. Go in the back, or better still, the side. (p. 35)*

His other trick is to attempt to shock, for example in the discussion on the number of foreskins of Christ that had apparently been preserved at the time of the Reformation. He tells the boys that examiners will be bored by reading competent papers:

Key quotation

Irwin *Come the fourteen foreskins of Christ and they'll think they've won the pools. (p. 19)*

Later we see him in the latrine trenches at Rievaulx Abbey, where he claims that 'ancient arsewipes' (p. 59) hallowed by time are what really interests the public.

Bennett uses him to represent a particular kind of populist television historian. Posner refers to him as a 'celebrity' (p. 61), a word which for many has negative connotations. His later evolution to a slithery spin doctor is unsurprising.

Mrs Lintott is used to express a feminist view of history, which she feels has been the province of men for far too long. Women historians, she states, do not appear on TV, 'because they don't come bouncing up to you with every new historical notion they've come up with...the bow-wow school of history' (p. 84). Rudge, when asked for his definition of history, expresses his unenthusiastic view

Build critical skills

It has been suggested that Hector's death was not an accident but suicide. Given our knowledge of Bennett's view of history, do you think this is at all likely?

in comedic fashion. For him, history is 'just one fucking thing after another' (p. 85).

Bennett's exploration of the meaning of history also considers the complete and utter randomness of events. This is illustrated first by the exposure of Hector's 'fiddling', simply because the Headmaster's wife happens to see him out of a window while she is working at Age Concern on a Wednesday afternoon. She does not normally work on a Wednesday, and if a customer had come in or the traffic lights had changed, she might have missed the entire incident.

As well as that, Dakin explains to Irwin that in 1940, Halifax rather than Churchill was the first choice for the post of prime minister during the war years but that Halifax was at the dentist on the afternoon that the decision was taken and that therefore the job went to Churchill:

Key quotation

Dakin *If Halifax had had better teeth we might have lost the war. (p. 90)*

These two incidents prepare us for the eventual random accident to Hector and Irwin at the end of the play. If the Headmaster had not come in at that precise moment and told Hector to take Irwin instead, the outcome might have been very different.

Sex and sexuality

Various ideas about sex and sexuality also underpin the play. The boys' enactment of the French brothel scene is a playful and hilarious introduction to their take on gender politics, but in the main, Bennett presents a somewhat bleak picture of sexual relationships. The introduction of the idea of prostitution, with its foregrounding of material gain over genuine feelings and values, may also be a reference to Irwin's attitude to knowledge and its effect on the boys. For example, it could be said that Posner prostitutes his true feelings when he plays down his real feelings about the Holocaust in his university entrance paper.

Sexist attitudes were not uncommon in the 1980s and perhaps not unexpectedly, flourish in the predominantly male atmosphere of the school. For example, Bennett presents Dakin's pursuit of Fiona using the imagery of war, as if she is the enemy, merely a country to be conquered. He describes her as his 'Western Front', with every inch of territory being 'hotly contested' (p. 28). Later in the play, he somewhat ungallantly informs Scripps of his progress:

Key quotation

Dakin *Broke through. Had the Armistice. The Treaty of Versailles. It's now the Weimar Republic. (p. 81)*

All of this suggests little respect for Fiona as a person, particularly as at the start of the play he articulated his desire to have sex with her on the floor of the Headmaster's study, subverting the Headmaster's mantra that 'one should have targets' (p. 22). Dakin has merely used her for his own selfish purposes and to prove his masculine prowess. Possibly because of his experience on the motorbike with Hector, he does recognise the vulnerabilities of being female:

Key quotation

Dakin *Lecher though one is, or aspires to be, it occurs to me that the lot of women cannot be easy, who must suffer such inexpert male fumblings virtually on a daily basis. (p. 77)*

However, he does not seem troubled by this. Bennett is exploring the effects of typical 'laddish' attitudes although it is interesting to note that towards the end of the play, Dakin appears to be more excited by the idea of seducing Irwin.

Rudge, too, is presented as someone who sees women as nothing more than a pleasant, relaxing hobby, of lesser importance than sport. He states that he has sex only on Fridays because he 'needs the weekend free for 'rugger. And golf' (p. 22). Here Bennett may be satirising the sexual attitudes of many dedicated sports fans.

The Headmaster too harasses Fiona, suggesting his lack of respect for her. Furthermore, Dakin's remark that he 'chases her round the table trying to cop a feel' (p. 29) suggests that Dakin sees it in comedic terms, almost like a sketch from a farce or a 1970s television sketch show, again showing lack of concern for Fiona's feelings. He uses his knowledge of the Headmaster's behaviour as a way to blackmail him in order to get Hector reinstated.

Only Mrs Lintott questions their casual sexist assumptions, reminding the boys that they may be interviewed by a woman at Oxbridge, and explaining that the reason there are no female historians on television is that history is not such a 'frolic' for women as it is for men.

Marriage is generally presented as a fairly unsatisfactory state. Mrs Lintott's view of Hector's 'somewhat unexpected wife' (p. 41) is that she, like many women, is someone who wants 'a husband on a low light…the man's lukewarm attentions just what they married them for' (p. 92). Instead of a deeply satisfying intimacy, their marriage is characterised by distance and pretence. This is confirmed by Hector who claims his wife is unlikely to be interested in his activity with the boys.

Mrs Lintott's marriage does not appear to have been happy either, since he was a man who 'told stories' and 'legged it to Dumfries' (p. 22).

Build critical skills

'They never get round the conference table. In 1919, for instance, they just arranged the flowers then gracefully retired.' (p. 85)

What do you understand by Mrs Lintott's comment, and what point do you think Bennett is making?

Perhaps this lack of marital bliss is unsurprising given the nature of the attitudes to women that are presented in the play.

Furthermore, the Headmaster tells Mrs Lintott that after finding a reason for sacking Hector, he was so pleased that his wife, who he refers to as Mrs Armstrong 'was startled to find she was the object of unaccustomed sexual interference herself' (p. 68).

Neither do homosexual relationships seem to bring the characters happiness and fulfilment. Hector has spent a lifetime in a sham marriage, having grown up at a time when homosexual acts between men were against the law and subject to quite vicious public condemnation. Because of this, he has been obliged to suppress his sexuality, which may have led to his inappropriate feelings for young boys. He tells Irwin that in the past a boy or boys did make him unhappy but advises Irwin to stop short of touching one, lest the boy think him a fool:

Key quotation

See it as an inoculation, rather. Briefly painful but providing immunity for however long it takes. With the occasional booster...another face, a reminder of the pain...it can last you half a lifetime. (p. 94)

He has spent his life getting by on the occasional 'fiddle' of boys who tolerate rather than enjoy the attention, seeing it as just another aspect of his eccentricity. Post revelations about Jimmy Savile, we understandably tend to view this kind of behaviour as much more sinister and damaging than in Bennett's presentation of it here. In this particular case, Bennett encourages us towards a more lighthearted approach, having pointed out in interviews that the boys are 17 or 18, and that they go with Hector willingly. Nor is there any suggestion that these boys feel that they have been damaged by the experience. In fact, the only boy who seems damaged in adulthood is Posner, who is not invited to go on the bike. As always, as a student of the play, it is important that you make up your own mind on the seriousness of the abuse.

Irwin too remains 'in the closet'. He does not say anything of his own experience to Posner when the boy comes to him for advice. However, when Dakin propositions him, despite initial reluctance, he weakens and accepts, although the meeting never takes place since Dakin 'couldn't face the wheelchair' (p. 106). This suggests that Dakin's admiration for Irwin was somewhat superficial.

Only Posner is able to be honest about his sexuality. His 'spaniel heart' pines for Dakin but 'Posner's reward', when it comes, is inevitably disappointing in that it consists of a brief hug, while Posner was hoping for something 'more...lingering' (p. 103). At the end of the play we are told that he is alone and mentally fragile, and that the only friends he has made are 'on the internet and none in his right name or even gender' (p.108).

> **GRADE** *BOOSTER*
>
> Turn to the Top ten quotations section for short memorable quotations on the main themes. You may find it very useful to have them at your fingertips in the examination.

Motif

A motif is an idea or object that recurs throughout a literary work. It is different from a theme which is a central idea, but it may be used to enhance our understanding of other themes and ideas. An important motif in *The History Boys* is the motif of war.

The motif of war

In the Language section (pp. 56–61), you will see that there are a number of metaphorical references to war. However, in addition to that, there are several direct references to war itself throughout the play.

For example, when the Head and Irwin interrupt the French lesson which is set in a brothel, the focus switches from sex to war as the Head is presented with a hilarious representation of suffering in a First World War military hospital.

In Irwin's lesson with the boys on the poetry of the First World War, he disparages the accepted view that the First World War was a tragedy and that the war poets such as Siegfried Sassoon and Wilfred Owen felt revulsion and horror which they expressed through some of the finest war poetry ever written. He tells them that both men were 'surprisingly bloodthirsty' (p. 26). It is difficult to find any evidence of this view in their actual poetry. This does not worry Irwin, who uses it as an opportunity to persuade the boys that they need a new 'angle', regardless of truth.

The boys' response is to recite Larkin's poem 'MCMXIV' (1914 being the year that the First World War broke out), a poem which highlights both the lost innocence and the tragedy of war that Irwin attempts to reduce to an 'angle'. Maurice Rutherford, the Hull-born poet writing on the Philip Larkin society's website (**www.philiplarkin.com**), has this to say about the loss of innocence in the poem:

> '...because of censorship and the slow speed of communications, much of the innocence back home in Blighty lasted for most of the four year conflict, until the truth could no longer be withheld or ignored when the blinded, gassed or otherwise maimed returned to various homelands, leaving behind their thousands of 'fallen' comrades.'

Key quotation

Scripps *But it's all true.*

Irwin *What has that got to do with it? What has that got to do with anything? (p. 24)*

Build critical skills

How do you respond to the boys' reading of 'MCMXIV'? Do you accept Irwin's version of truth or the 'truth' expressed in the poem?

Timm's last line, 'Never such innocence again' (p. 27) of course can be interpreted as Bennett's comment on the boys being about to embark on life, as well as the young men in the poem discovering the horrific truth about war.

Irwin's argument that Haig should have the unknown soldier disinterred and shot all over again for giving comfort to the enemy is counterpointed by Posner's recitation of 'Drummer Hodge', and the idea that 'lost boy though he is on the other side of the world, he still has a name...' (p. 55). Bennett is perhaps showing us that, as Scripps says to Irwin, 'You can't explain away the poetry...' (p. 27).

Irwin's dispassionate dissection of the Holocaust highlights the distinction between Irwin's 'distance' and Hector's more passionate stance:

Key quotation

Hector *Why can you not simply condemn the camps outright as an unprecedented horror?* (p. 73)

We can also see that the boys, with the exception of Scripps and Posner at this stage, are moving towards the Irwin approach, as Lockwood argues that the death camps should be put 'in proportion'.

Scripps's reference to Irwin's later demonstration on television that Roosevelt was the real culprit when the Japanese bombed Pearl Harbor creates comedy in its ludicrousness, but also serves to demonstrate the extremes of Irwin's approach.

Even 'Wish Me Luck as You Wave Me Goodbye', which the boys sing as they set off for Oxbridge, can be seen as an oblique reference to war. Although written and recorded before the Second World War, it became popular during the war and was often associated with putting on a brave face as men were going off to fight and facing an uncertain future.

GRADE *FOCUS*

Grade 5

To achieve Grade 5, students should reveal a clear understanding of the key themes of the play and how Bennett uses language, form and structure to explore them, supported by appropriate references to the text.

Grade 8

To achieve Grade 8, students will be able to examine and evaluate the key themes of the play, analysing the ways that Bennett uses language, form and structure to explore them. Comments will be supported by carefully chosen and well-integrated references to the text.

REVIEW YOUR LEARNING

1 Why, according to Hector, should students learn poetry by heart?

2 How does Hector refer to CVs?

3 What is the name of the poem that Hector and Posner discuss?

4 Who says 'You can't explain away the poetry'?

5 How does Hector being caught fiddling demonstrate the random nature of events?

6 How does Mrs Lintott challenge the sexist assumptions of the men in the play?

7 How does Dakin manage to get Hector reinstated?

8 What happened to Mrs Lintott's husband?

9 Who has a 'spaniel heart'?

10 Which poem do the boys recite to counter Irwin's disparagement of their views on the First World War?

Answers on p. 103.

Target your thinking

- How does Bennett tell the story of *The History Boys* to his audience? (**AO2**)
- What techniques does Bennett use to make the staging of the play effective? (**AO2**)
- How does Bennett use dialogue in the play? (**AO2**)

You will notice from the questions above that when analysing language and style, the Assessment Objective with which we are most concerned is AO2, which refers to the writer's methods and is usually highlighted in the exam question by the word 'how'. It is of vital importance since it is the medium through which writers help to create our understanding of plot, character and themes.

Examiners report that AO2 is often the most overlooked by students in the examination. For example, candidates who fail to address AO2 often write about the characters in a play as if they are real people involved in real events rather than analysing them as 'constructs' or creations of the writer.

To succeed at AO2, you must deal effectively with the writer's use of language, form and structure.

Form

Very simply, the form of *The History Boys* is that of a play with two Acts, each framed by a flash-forward to Irwin. In Act One we see the rise of Irwin and the beginnings of Hector's decline, while Act Two sees Hector's decline accelerate, the boys' success and the final twist of the accident at the end. There are certain dramatic conventions associated with the play form, such as stage directions, sets, stage props, music and of course, dialogue. The decisions that a playwright makes about all those different aspects are closely related to both the structure and the language of the play. Turn to p. 15 for analysis of the structure of *The History Boys*.

Stage directions

Obviously, when watching the play on stage, the audience is not aware of what might be in the stage directions. Stage directions are there to help an actor or a reader to interpret what might be going on, to mark exits and entrances, to indicate a particular action by a character, to show how the playwright might want the actor to deliver a particular line or to make clear what the playwright might have wanted in terms of lighting or props.

Although there is some use of stage directions in *The History Boys*, Bennett uses them quite sparingly and certainly does not show a great deal of interest in props or lighting to create atmosphere. The lack of props, like the minimal set, encourages the audience to focus on the words and actions of the actors. *The History Boys* is, in terms of language, quite dense; it is a play in which the audience needs to concentrate above all on what is being said on stage.

However, Bennett does use directions to tell us when Irwin is in a wheelchair and thus helps to locate the time period within the play. Directions are also used to introduce the motif of war, when the boys remove Hector's motorcycle clothes. The boys name each item in French, presenting it to the audience 'with a flourish' (p. 4). These actions might recall a group of young squires divesting a warrior or knight of his armour. However, they are also a quick indication of Hector's unusual and flamboyant style.

This section indicates the importance of Hector in the play, the particular relationship he has with the boys and perhaps hints at the ideological battle to follow, where Hector's ideas on education bring him into direct conflict with Irwin and the Headmaster. When we are told that Hector has an air of 'studied eccentricity' and that he wears 'a bow tie' (p. 4), it is clear that we are in no ordinary classroom.

Stage directions sometimes indicate action such as '*He hits them on the head with an exercise book*' (p. 5) but they also interpret action, for example when Hector puts out a hand towards Posner during their tutorial and '*for a moment it almost seems as if Posner will take it, or even that Hector might put it on Posner's knee. But the moment passes*' (p. 56).

A number of short musical interludes which help to create the distinctive atmosphere of the play are also indicated through stage directions.

Set

The set is fairly limited in that most of the action takes place in the classroom of a boys' school in the 1980s in the north of England. This can be used to help to create the sense of a closed world, possibly a microcosm of England in the 1980s featuring two opposing sides of an ideological divide.

However, it could also support Bennett's hope that the issues of the play may be of interest outside of a specific time period. There is nothing on stage which might be described as strong period detail: the boys wear uniform which would not be likely to change a great deal over several years or even decades.

When writing the play, Bennett admits that he did not pay a great deal of attention to when it was set because, for him, it was about 'two sorts of teaching — or two teachers, anyway…' (Introduction to the play p. xix) Bennett has stated that he regards the actual characters to be of greater importance than the themes.

In the introduction to the Faber edition, Bennett explains that he does not include many notes on stage directions or changes of scene in order to keep the action fluid. In performance, other scenes, such as the staffroom or Headmaster's office, are often achieved by the use of sliding walls.

Time shifts

In addition, the framing device of Irwin in a wheelchair, several years after the main action of the play, which appears in an unspecified location at the beginning of Act One, suggests his role as an outsider. The same character is shown in what had been the latrine in the ruins of Rievaulx abbey, a part of an outside broadcast where he explains to camera how medieval monks wiped their bottoms, an 'angle' which is very typically Irwin.

Video clips

The use of video clips projected onto a screen at the rear of the stage is not generally specified either, but again they are usually used in performance as the action shifts from one place to another, to enrich the sense of the world of the school and beyond and perhaps to explore some of Bennett's ideas. In addition, projected shots of Hector as a young man during the memorial service are particularly moving, since it reminds us that he too was once as young and innocent as the History Boys. Of course, this also poignantly reminds us that they too will one day be as he is now.

Use of song

Music is used to create atmosphere and sometimes to aid the move from one scene to another. For example, Posner sings 'some [Edith] Piaf' (p. 12) as we move into the French lesson. Piaf's music evokes both France itself through her iconic status and also the backdrop of her struggles with tragedy. The atmosphere of the 'brothel' is further enhanced when Scripps plays 'La Vie en Rose', the name of a brothel where Piaf sometimes sang, as well as the name of her signature song.

On other occasions, song is used to express heartfelt emotion as in Posner's angst-ridden rendition of 'Bewitched, Bothered and Bewildered' for Dakin, the camp classic 'Wish Me Luck As You Wave Me Goodbye' as the boys leave for Oxbridge or their touching version of 'Bye, Bye Blackbird' at Hector's memorial service.

The 'fourth wall'

There are a number of examples of characters breaking the 'fourth wall'. The fourth wall does not exist in reality. When in a theatre watching a play, we might say that there is an imaginary wall between the actors and the audience, which we term 'the fourth wall'. The actors keep up a pretence that they cannot see the audience and the audience watch the action of the play as if they were 'a fly on the wall'.

'Breaking the fourth wall' occurs when characters step out from the action of the play and address the audience directly. You may be able to think of examples when Shakespeare uses this technique, such as at the end of *A Midsummer Night's Dream* or the prologue of *Henry V*. It was used in the twentieth century by the playwright Brecht who wanted audiences to think about the issues in a play, rather than react emotionally, so he used it to destroy the illusion of realism on stage. It is not used very often in modern stage plays, although you might see examples on film or television in programmes such as *House of Cards* and even *Mrs Brown's Boys*.

Both Timms and Scripps look back on events from the position of adults, for example when Timms informs the audience that 'The hitting never hurt. It was a joke. None of us cared' (p. 7). Notice the switch into the past tense, which separates it from the rest of the action. Scripps in particular is used by Bennett almost as a narrator in the play, filling in the audience on details to do with Irwin's later notoriety as a historian, for example, and establishing a connection of trust with the audience:

Key quotation

Scripps *...he would one day demonstrate on television that those who had been genuinely caught napping by the attack on Pearl Harbor were the Japanese... (p. 35)*

When Mrs Lintott suddenly addresses the audience at the end of the interview with the Headmaster where he spells out for her what Hector has done, the effect is to suddenly dislodge us from our comfort zone and to make us pay attention to what she is saying about her role as a woman within the school and the nature of men which she sees as essentially childish and selfish:

Key quotation

Mrs Lintott *I have not hitherto been allotted an inner voice, my role a patient and not unamused sufferance of the predilections and preoccupations of men. They kick their particular stone along the street and I watch. (p. 68)*

Language
Dialogue

When looking at the language in a play, we are principally concerned with dialogue. Dialogue refers to the words spoken by the actors. It can be used in a number of ways including to move the action forward, reveal character, create humour, pathos or atmosphere and to introduce and develop themes. Bennett's use of dialogue has a number of distinctive features.

Naturalistic dialogue

Sometimes, Bennett uses naturalistic dialogue, for instance in the simple vocabulary and everyday speech patterns of Rudge during the mock interviews:

Key quotation

Rudge *Look I'm shit at all this. Sorry. If they like me and they want to take me they'll take me because I'm dull and ordinary. (p. 86)*

Slang and idiom are also, on occasions, features of the boys' speech, particularly, although not exclusively, when they speak among themselves. This is a normal feature of adolescent speech especially when in informal situations. Dakin tells Scripps that the Headmaster chases Fiona 'hoping to cop a feel' (p. 29), that while on the bike with Hector he wishes that Hector would 'just go for it' (p. 21) and that the room he stayed in during the Oxbridge trip belonged to someone who Dakin thought was 'a bit of a pillock' (p. 96). Scripps declares that 'God should get real' (p. 45), Posner tells Irwin that the other boys are 'taking the piss' (p. 39) and Rudge describes himself as a 'thick sod' (p. 97).

All this serves to remind us that despite their extremely stylised speech elsewhere, these boys are ordinary teenagers, and their typical use of slang and idiom emphasises their youth and vulnerability.

The use of nicknames for each other by Scripps (Scrippsy) and Posner (Poz) suggests their supportive friendship. Mrs Lintott tells Irwin, who does not have one, that nicknames are a sign of affection. Hector's real name is Douglas, but his nickname Hector is perhaps more appropriate in that it informs us of how the boys see him at the start of the play. It recalls the heroic Greek warrior, who the historian James Redfield describes as '...a martyr to loyalties, a witness to the things of this world, a hero ready to die for the precious imperfections of ordinary life' (*Nature and Culture in the Iliad*, p. xi). The trustworthy Scripps refers to him at the beginning and towards the end of the play as 'the big man' (p. 7 and p. 77), a name which suggests not only physically large, but also perhaps large in heart, mind and stature.

Mrs Lintott, who also appears to be liked by the boys, is 'Tot or Totty' which she views as ironic, since Totty is a slang, sexist term for an attractive woman.

Characters such as the Headmaster have distinctive speech patterns. His early speeches when he articulates his ambitions for the boys suggest lazy sound bites or half-formed ideas. The line 'Think charm. Think polish. Think Renaissance man' (p. 9) suggests his superficial nature and his limited understanding of the nature of education.

Similarly, when he is speaking to Irwin, a series of short dogmatic phrases suggests his lack of genuine concern for the boys, unless, in his opinion, they enhance the school's reputation. His complete and utter dismissal of Rudge shows a lack of recognition of Rudge's other strengths and his value as a person:

Key quotation

Headmaster *They are a likely lot, the boys. All keen. One oddity. Rudge. Determined to try for Oxford and Christ Church of all places. No hope. (p. 11)*

His cliché-ridden speech at Hector's memorial service with its hackneyed use of metaphor and false sentiment suggests a shallow mind and a hypocritical nature.

This contrasts with the beautifully simple, honest statements by the boys, each of whom seems to speak from the heart, in that they acknowledge Hector's flaws but still hold him in high regard:

Key quotation

Crowther *He was stained and shabby and did unforgivable things but he led you to expect the best. Even his death was a lesson and added to the store. (p. 107)*

Taboo language

Bennett often uses taboo language to help to reflect character, for example the sexual language used by Dakin and the down-to-earth nature of Rudge's definition of history. Perhaps more surprising is Mrs Lintott's language when she insults the Headmaster using vulgar terms for female genitalia. This, however, is spoken to the audience, suggesting that she is speaking from the heart and outside of the normal conventions of her life as a teacher. At other times she uses euphemism. For example, she mentions that Dakin is 'seeing' Fiona and asks if Wittgenstein travelled 'on the other bus...' (p. 84) (a slang expression for enquiring if he was homosexual).

She is more relaxed with Hector telling him that his description of his fiddling as a 'laying on' of hands is 'colossal balls' (p. 95). However, she perhaps indicates her instinctive sympathy for him when she scolds him for his behaviour, because she self-censors to produce the mild expletive: 'You...twerp' (p. 95).

The Headmaster's use of expletives may suggest that he is lost for words, for example, after having been outflanked during the French lesson, when Hector refuses to give up any of his teaching time to Irwin. He uses expletives again, having lost his temper with Hector, when cursing the Renaissance, 'and literature and Plato and Michelangelo and Oscar Wilde and all the other shrunken violets you people line up' (p. 53). At the very least, this suggests poor man management skills and possibly homophobia, although it might also be argued that he is referring here to relationships between adults and minors rather than homosexuality as such.

Irwin's final line to Dakin before driving off with Hector perhaps reflects the freedom he has now found to speak as he feels, when he too uses profane language.

Stylised dialogue

Have you noticed that you often can't think of a witty reply to something that has been said to you until afterwards? The French call this kind of frustrating afterthought *l'esprit de l'escalier* ('the staircase wit', suggesting that you only think of a great retort as you reach the bottom of the stairs on your way out).

In *The History Boys*, as well as naturalistic speech, Bennett also uses stylised dialogue so that the boys often speak with great eloquence and knowledge. With the possible exception of Rudge in the mock interview, Bennett never presents these teenagers as mumbling, inarticulate or lost for words. There are no *l'esprit de l'escalier* moments.

Nick Hytner, who directed the original production as well as the film version, states: 'Alan Bennett is a stylist as recognisable, in his way, as Oscar Wilde. People don't actually talk the way they do in his plays: the "history boys" are often far wittier and more articulate than even the cleverest Oxbridge entrant...' (*Guardian*, 15 September 2006).

This can be seen, for example, in Scripps's witty comment to Dakin in respect of Fiona, 'Just let us know when you get to Berlin' (p. 29), in Timms's and Lockwood's challenge to Irwin on the idea that art can be expressed 'in other words', or the philosophical discussion the boys have with Irwin and Hector about whether the Holocaust should be taught.

Dakin's expression is often sophisticated, such as in his comments on 'inexpert male fumblings' (p. 77) or when Irwin returns the boys' work by throwing it at them:

Key quotation

Dakin *Actually, sir, I know tradition requires it of the eccentric schoolmaster, but do you mind not throwing the books? They tend to fall apart.* (p. 18)

Scripps too can be unexpectedly lyrical. For instance, when discussing with Dakin why Hector's lifts have stopped, he cleverly integrates a quotation from Matthew Arnold's poem 'Dover Beach'.

Build critical skills

Scripps *No more the bike's melancholy long withdrawing roar as he dropped you at the corner, your honour still intact.* (p. 77)

If at times the boys' speech does not sound like teenage boys, does it matter? Does it affect your enjoyment of the play either positively or negatively?

With Irwin, there is often a sense of performance. In the first scene, which is also the audience's first impression of him, he is actually advising MPs on performance.

At other times, his speech is clearly an actual performance, for example in the opening of Act Two where he is presenting a history programme in the grounds of a ruined monastery, neatly explaining that 'there is an increment even in excrement' (p. 59).

The scene opens with a rehashing of something which sounds slick but which does not stand up to closer scrutiny. He used the same lines about Henry VIII on the boys in Act One (p. 35), suggesting that there is little genuine feeling in anything he says:

Key quotation

Irwin *If you want to learn about Stalin, study Henry VIII.*

If you want to learn about Mrs Thatcher, study Henry VIII.

If you want to learn about Hollywood, study Henry VIII. (pp. 35 and 58)

Build critical skills

'I would try not to be shrill or earnest. An amused tolerance always comes over best, particularly on television.' (p. 3)

How does Bennett's presentation of Irwin in these lines help you to understand him as a character?

On this occasion, he admits that his style is 'meretricious' or 'Eye-catching, showy; false' (p. 60), as it always was. Bennett's use of the word 'meretricious' may be quite telling because its Latin stem originally referred to prostitution, suggesting that Irwin is up for hire and willing to prostitute his talents. His delivery is characteristically confident until he stumbles over his lines in his awareness that he is being observed by an adult Posner.

His dialogue when confronted by Dakin about his time at university is evasive. He only speaks directly when pushed to by Dakin, when they arrange their assignation and Irwin appears to choose sex over research into a monastery:

Hector's speech with the boys also has an air of performance, such as the 'elaborate pantomime' (p. 6) that goes on over his hitting them and their pretending to mind, and his affectionate verbal abuse, such as when he calls Timms a 'Foul, festering grubby-minded little trollop' (p. 5). However, when it comes to literature and history, Bennett shows us a man who is always passionate and always genuine in his passion. This is most clearly seen in the warmth, humanity and depth shown in Hector's discussion with Posner on 'Drummer Hodge'.

intertextuality: the referencing of other texts with the idea that your understanding of one text can be enhanced by knowledge of another text

Intertextuality abounds in Hector's speech and establishes him as erudite, eloquent and sophisticated. For example, the extract from King Lear in Act One deepens our understanding of *The History Boys* because it foreshadows the downfall and death of Hector.

Much of the intertextuality is expressed through Hector's recital of poetry that he has encouraged the boys to memorise. This is because Hector sees it as 'the antidote' to what happens in life:

Build critical skills

Hector continues by again quoting A. E. Housman:

To think that two and two are four

And never five or three

The heart of man has long been sore

And long 'tis like to be.

With reference to his behaviour on the motorcycle, what do you understand by Hector's observation here?

For Hector, perhaps unfulfilled by the circumstances of his day-to-day existence, literature is seen as a reliable source of comfort and guidance. For example, when the Headmaster tackles him on the subject of his fiddling, he quotes A. E. Housman:

> The tree of man was never quiet:
> Then 'twas the Roman; now 'tis I. (p. 52)

The Headmaster challenges him with 'This is no time for poetry'. Hector's reply, 'I would have thought it was just the time', is very telling in that it signals his dependence on its consoling wisdom.

In addition, Bennett also uses Hector's many references to poets, playwrights and thinkers to establish his sensitivity, perceptiveness and the depth and breadth of his knowledge. He is contrasted with Irwin, who only appreciates 'gobbets' that might come in useful in an examination.

Intertextuality is also used by Bennett to widen the intellectual and cultural spectrum of the play. However, it is important to note that its use is never random. It adds layers of meaning in a range of ways. When Posner sings 'Bewitched, Bothered and Bewildered', it adds to our understanding of his emotional state.

It is also used to tell us something about the relationship between Hector and the boys, when for instance they copy his habit of using quotations. The fact that Lockwood quotes Pascal, and Dakin quotes W. H. Auden, when challenging Irwin during his first lesson, is an indication of their admiration and loyalty towards Hector. Their participation in the film game, with scenes from Hector's era is surely a humouring of their teacher which continues until the end of the play, when Rudge sings 'It's a Sin' by the Pet Shop Boys and collects the money.

Themes and ideas are further developed through intertextuality, such as when Posner and Scripps enact the scene from *Brief Encounter*, a film about a secret love affair, which links to the forbidden expressions of sexuality in the play or in the quoting of 'MCMXIV' which links to the loss of innocence and the boys' unpreparedness for the future.

Humour

Although the subject of *The History Boys* is a serious one, it is the combination of sadness and humour that most audiences remember. As the singer Morrissey said of Alan Bennett in an interview published by Len Brown Omnibus Press in 2010:

> 'He's so terribly funny that when he writes a line full of biting sadness it cuts through all the more.'

Bennett is often spoken of as having a peculiarly northern sensibility in the type of humour he uses. As well as the link between tragedy and comedy, northern humour is often associated with the deflating of pomposity.

Bennett has a particularly sharp ear for absurdity, particularly **bathos**, which is shown most clearly in some of the Headmaster's lines.

bathos: comedic technique which involves an abrupt transition in style from the lofty to the commonplace, having a ludicrous effect

For example, the Headmaster waxes lyrical about his aspirations for the school and then wonders whether one of the names he has mentioned is in fact, a prison:

Key quotation

Headmaster *I want to see us up there with Manchester Grammar School, Haberdashers' Aske's. Leighton Park. Or is that an open prison? No matter. (p. 11)*

Furthermore, he describes himself as 'corseted by the curriculum' (p. 11) a metaphor which conjures up a ludicrously inappropriate image and establishes him as a figure of fun so that later when he rebukes Hector

▲ Film poster for *The Seventh Veil*, 1945

with the words, 'A hand on a boy's genitals at fifty miles an hour and you call it nothing?' (p. 53), it is hard not to laugh, even though we probably agree with him.

The boys' sex chat, where Dakin and Scripps discuss the topic of masturbation, inhabits a well-established comedic convention of males speaking frankly to each other, often on a limited range of subjects, when out of the earshot of females.

The enactment of excerpts by the boys from melodramatic films is amusing, partly because the dialogue to us sounds affected and theatrical, particularly when delivered in comic fashion by teenage boys. This can be illustrated in the clip from the 1945 film *The Seventh Veil*, where Scripps is playing the piano in role as Francesca.

Key quotation

Dakin *Francesca. You belong to me. We must always be together. You know that, don't you? Promise you'll stay with me always. Promise.*

She slowly shakes her head.

Very well. If that's the way you want it. If you won't play for me, you shan't play for anybody ever again.

He brings his stick down across her fingers on the keyboard. She shrieks and rushes sobbing from the room. (p. 66)

Build critical skills

'*For each and every one of you, his pupils, he opened a deposit account in the bank of literature and made you all shareholders in that wonderful world of words.*' (p. 106)

What does this extract tell us about the Headmaster and his values? Are you appalled, amused or both?

At other points, the humour is derived from Bennett's ear for the niceties of the meanings of language. For example, when Posner tells Irwin that some of 'the literature' suggests that his homosexual feelings will pass, he is referring to pamphlets or medical information for adolescents distributed at a time when at least some of the medical establishment held negative opinions towards homosexuality.

Irwin comments that he wanted to tell Posner that 'the literature may say that, but literature doesn't' (p. 42). This is flattering and amusing for an audience who understand the allusion to literature in the classical sense which generally illustrates a different view.

Irony

When the Headmaster delivers the memorial speech for Hector, the irony of his words coupled with the inappropriate banking metaphor is hugely revealing, since Hector has earlier been heard to say that he never wanted to turn out boys who 'in later life had a deep love of literature' (p. 94).

There are a number of other examples of **situational irony**. For example, Rudge is the only character who was offered a place on the day of the interview and yet he was the one initially referred to by the Headmaster as having 'No hope' (p. 11). The fact that he was actually 'just what the college rugger team needed' (p. 98) mocks not only the Headmaster but also the skewed values of the university's admissions policy.

Dakin's comment to Irwin on their assignation, 'And we're not in the subjunctive either. It is going to happen' (p. 102), is ironic since it clearly does not happen. **Dramatic irony** occurs in the scene when Hector puts his head on the desk and weeps in despair. The audience realises that this is because he has to leave his beloved post as a teacher, having been spotted 'fiddling' by the Headmaster's wife. The boys, however, are unaware of what has happened and are unsure how to deal with a distraught Hector. This creates audience sympathy since they are aware of Hector's isolation and the fact that the boys are unwittingly tormenting him, although they themselves may believe that they are merely teasing.

Perhaps the most interesting use of irony in the play is in Scripps's speech just prior to the accident and after he anticipates a happy ending for all.

> **situational irony:** when the outcome is the opposite of what one might have expected

> **dramatic irony:** when the audience is aware of something when the characters on stage are not

Build critical skills

Scripps *Actually I shouldn't have said everybody's happy, as just saying the words meant, like in a play, that the laws of irony were thereby activated and things began to unravel pretty quickly after that. (p. 103)*

Why is Scripps's speech supremely ironic? How do you think it would affect an audience?

Imagery

In the Themes section of this guide (pp. 41–51), there is a discussion on the number of historical or literary references to actual war in the play. However, on a number of occasions, Bennett uses the language of war **metaphorically** to create certain effects.

For example, Hector describes exams as 'the enemy of education' (p. 48). His classroom door is locked against 'the Forces of Progress' (p. 36). When Dakin fails to arrive for the poetry tutorial with Hector and Posner, Hector's comment is, 'we must carry on the fight without him' (p. 54). Akthar describes their lessons as 'the rapier cut and thrust' (p. 64) and just before Hector puts his head on the desk in despair, he tells the boys that sometimes they 'defeat' him (p. 64). These references create and develop the sense of a beleaguered Hector at war with the rest of the educational world.

After the discussion of 'Drummer Hodge' and the arrival of Dakin, Hector states, 'And now, having thrown in Drummer Hodge as found, here reporting for duty, helmet in hand, is young Lieutenant Dakin' (p. 56). The **double entendre** does not distract us from the obvious link between Dakin (and Posner too) with poor Drummer Hodge.

> **metaphorically:** not literally; by means of a metaphor. A metaphor is a comparison which does not use 'like' or 'as' but instead says something is something else

> **double entendre:** a word or phrase that in a particular context may have a double meaning, and the second meaning may be sexual

Faced with the reality of boys as young as he was, the young soldier's fate is more poignant, and we are aware that Posner, like the drummer, is too young and unprepared for the battles he must face. Dakin, on the other hand, may do very well.

In addition, Dakin's seduction of Fiona is described using the metaphor of war.

Build critical skills

Dakin *I mean, just as moving up to the front-line troops had to pass the sites of previous battles where every inch of territory has been hotly contested, so it is with me...like particularly her tits, which only fell after a prolonged campaign three weeks ago and to which I now have immediate access... (p. 28)*

How does Bennett's use of metaphor reveal Dakin's attitude to Fiona in this extract and what is its effect? Identify the use of bathos and its effect.

Interestingly, Bennett uses another metaphor from warfare in Dakin's references to the Nazi invasion of Poland, when attempting to seduce Irwin. In linking Dakin to Hitler, Bennett clearly presents Dakin as the character with the power in this exchange.

Other examples of imagery include Irwin's clichéd comment that the more privileged students that the History Boys will be competing against will have been 'groomed like thoroughbreds' (p. 20) conjures up a world of precious pampering and training, but also suggests a fiercely competitive race for young animals, where the kudos goes to the owners and trainers.

It contrasts rather with the somewhat undignified extended metaphor developed by Mrs Lintott and Rudge describing him as a 'battery chicken':

Key quotation

Rudge *You've force-fed us the facts; now we're in the process of running around acquiring flavour... (p. 33)*

More striking perhaps is Mrs Lintott's comment that 'History is women following behind with the bucket' (p. 85) which reflects her disillusionment with men, the idea that women have only been allowed to follow rather than lead and that women clean up the mess that men make.

Other examples include Scripps's comment when the Headmaster enters at the precise moment when Dakin is about to accompany Hector on the back of the bike, and tells Hector to take Irwin instead:

Key quotation

Scripps *And here history rattled over the points... (p. 105)*

This metaphor is effective because it describes the moment when the unstoppable train of history is suddenly diverted to a completely different track and in an instant everything changes, much as in Dakin's story about how we might not have won the war if Halifax had had better teeth.

GRADE *BOOSTER*

Remember: it is not enough to simply identify the methods used by a writer. You must explore the effects on the audience of the use of these features.

GRADE *FOCUS*

Grade 5

To achieve Grade 5, students will show a clear appreciation of the methods Bennett uses to create effects for the reader, supported by appropriate references to the text.

Grade 8

To achieve Grade 8, students will explore and analyse the methods that Bennett uses to create effects for the reader, supported by carefully chosen and well-integrated references to the text.

REVIEW YOUR LEARNING

1 Give one reason why Bennett uses a minimal set.
2 What is Hector wearing which suggests an 'air of studied eccentricity' (p. 4)?
3 How does Bennett indicate that Timms is speaking outside of the action of the play, when he tells the audience that no one minded being hit?
4 What is the effect of the moments when the boys' speech seems naturalistic?
5 How does Bennett make the audience sit up and take note of what Mrs Lintott says to the audience about her role as a woman within the school?
6 What does Mrs Lintott call Hector which suggests that she thinks he is an idiot but she is still fond of him?
7 What do you understand by 'naturalistic dialogue'?
8 In what way is Irwin 'meretricious'?
9 What do you understand by 'intertextuality'?
10 What extended metaphor does Dakin use to describe his seduction of Fiona?

Answers on p. 103.

Target your thinking

- What sorts of questions will you have to answer?
- What is the best way to plan your answer?
- How can you improve your grade?
- What do you have to do to achieve the highest grade?

Your response to a question on *The History Boys* will be assessed in a 'closed book' English Literature examination, which means that you are not allowed to take copies of your chosen text into the examination room. Both AQA and WJEC Eduqas offer *The History Boys* as an examination text and the two boards test in different ways. It is vital that you know on which paper the post-1914 text will be, so that you can be well prepared on the day of the examination.

Whichever board you are studying, the table on page 67 explains which paper and section the play appears in and gives you information about the sort of question you will face and how you will be assessed.

Marking

The marking of your responses varies according to the board your school or you have chosen. Both exam boards will have a slightly different mark scheme, consisting of a ladder of levels. The marks you achieve in each part of the examination will be converted to your final overall grade. Grades are numbered from 1–9, with 9 being the highest.

It is important that you familiarise yourself with the relevant mark scheme(s) for your examination. After all, how can you do well unless you know exactly what is required?

Assessment Objectives for individual assessments are explained in the next section of the guide (see pp. 75–79).

Approaching the examination question

First impressions

First read the whole question and make sure you understand exactly what the task requires you to do. It is very easy in the highly pressured atmosphere of the examination room to misread a question and this

Exam board	AQA	WJEC Eduqas
Paper Section	Paper 2 Section A	Paper 2 Section A
Type of question	Traditional essay-style with two bullets for guidance.	Extract-based question requiring response to aspect of extract and response to the same or similar aspect in the play as a whole.
Closed book	Yes	Yes
Choice of question	Yes — choice of 2	No
Paper and section length	Paper 2: 2 hours 15 minutes. Section A: approximately 45 minutes.	Paper 2: 2 hours 30 minutes. Section A: approximately 45 minutes.
% of whole grade	20% literature grade	20% literature grade
AOs assessed	AO1 AO2 AO3 AO4	AO1 AO2 AO4
Is AO4 (SPaG) assessed in this section?	Yes: 4 marks out of a total of 34.	Yes: 5 marks out of a total of 40.

can be disastrous. Under no circumstances should you try to twist the question to the one that you have spent hours revising or the one that you did brilliantly on in your mock exam.

Are you being asked to think about how a character or theme is being presented? Make sure you know so that you will be able to sustain your focus later.

Look carefully at any bullet points you are given. They are there to help and guide you.

As you will have noticed in the table above, the two boards (AQA and WJEC Eduqas) that offer *The History Boys* as a text have very different question formats. AQA offers a choice of two traditional essay-style questions, each one including two bullet points for guidance. The questions are likely to focus on either a character or theme. WJEC Eduqas, on the other hand, asks a question offering a short extract as a starting point.

You may wish to begin by underlining keywords in the question, such as 'how' to remind you to write about methods and any other words which you feel will help you to focus on answering the question you are being asked. Below are examples of the question types from each examination board which have been annotated by students in this way.

SPaG: spelling, punctuation and grammar

AQA

05 How does Bennett use the character of <u>Irwin</u> to explore ideas about <u>education</u>?

Write about:

- <u>how</u> Bennett presents the <u>character</u> of Irwin
- <u>how</u> Bennett uses <u>Irwin</u> to explore ideas about <u>education</u>

[30 marks]

AO4 [4 marks]

WJEC Eduqas

You should use the extract below and your knowledge of the whole play to answer this question.

(The extract is printed in the Sample essays section on p. 88.)

Write about the <u>relationship</u> between <u>Hector</u> and <u>the boys</u> and <u>how</u> it is presented at <u>different points</u> in the play.

In your response you should:

- refer to the <u>extract</u> and the <u>play as a whole</u>;
- show your understanding of <u>characters</u> and <u>events</u> in the play.

[40 marks]

Five of this question's marks are allocated for accuracy in spelling, punctuation and the use of vocabulary and sentence structures.

Approaching the AQA question

Before choosing your question, read them both carefully and make sure you understand exactly what the tasks require you to do. An important word in both questions is likely to be 'how', which means that Bennett's methods will be crucial in your response. Think very carefully before deciding which question to attempt. Choose the question which gives you the best chance to impress the examiner with your depth of knowledge.

Approaching the WJEC Eduqas question

First read the passage carefully, trying to get an overview or general impression of what is going on and what or who is being described.

Now read the passage again, underlining or highlighting any words or short phrases that you think might be related to the focus of the question and are of special interest. For example, they might be surprising, unusual or amusing. You might have a strong emotional or analytical reaction to them or you might think that they are particularly clever or noteworthy.

These words/phrases may work together to produce a particular effect or to get you to think about a particular theme or to explore the methods the writer uses to present a character in a particular way for their own purposes. You may pick out examples of literary techniques, such as use of imagery or contrast, or sound effects, such as alliteration, or a particularly clever use of stagecraft. You may spot an unusual word order, sentence construction or use of punctuation. Don't forget to consider the effect of stage directions, if included, as well as dialogue. The important thing to remember is that when you start writing you must try to explain the effects created by these words/phrases or techniques and not simply identify what they mean. Above all, ensure that you are answering the question.

Planning your answer (AQA and WJEC Eduqas)

It is advisable to write a plan before you start writing your response to avoid repeating yourself or getting into a muddle. A plan is important because it helps you to gather and organise your thoughts, but it should consist of brief words and phrases. A plan is not a first draft. You will not have time to do this. In fact, if your plan consists of full sentences at all, you are probably eating into the time you have available for writing a really insightful and considered answer.

You may find it helpful to use a diagram of some sort — perhaps a spider diagram or flow chart. This may help you to keep your mind open to new ideas as you plan, so that you can slot them in. You could make a list instead. The important thing is to choose a method that works for you.

If you have made a spider diagram, arranging your thoughts is a simple matter of numbering the branches in the best possible order.

The other advantage of having a plan is that if you run out of time, the examiner can look at the plan and may be able to give you an extra mark or two based on what you were about to do next.

Writing your answer (AQA and WJEC Eduqas)

Now you are ready to start writing your answer. The first thing to remember is that you are working against the clock and so it is really important to use your time wisely.

It is possible that you may not have time to deal with all of the points you wish to make in your response. If you simply identify several language features or a handful of themes and ideas and make a brief comment on each, you will be working at a fairly low level. The idea is to select the ones that you find most interesting and develop them in a sustained and detailed manner. In order to move up the levels in the mark scheme, it is important to write a lot about a little, rather than a little about a lot.

You must also remember to address the whole question as you will be penalised if you fail to do so.

If you have any time left at the end of the examination, do not waste it! Check carefully that your meaning is clear and that you have done the very best that you can. Look back at your plan and check that you have included all your best points. Is there anything else you can add? Keep thinking until you are told to put your pen down.

Referring to the author and title

You can refer to Bennett either by name (make sure you spell it correctly) or as 'the writer'. You should never use his first name (Alan) as this sounds as if you know him personally. You can also save time by giving the play title in full the first time you refer to it, and afterwards simply referring to it as 'the play'.

GRADE *BOOSTER*

Do not lose sight of the writer in your response. Remember that the play is a construct — the characters, their thoughts, their words, their actions have all been created by Bennett — so most of your points need to be about what Bennett might have been trying to achieve. In explaining how his message is conveyed to you, for instance through an event, something about a character, use of symbolism, comedy, irony and so on, don't forget to mention his name. For example:

- Bennett makes it clear that xxx.
- It is evident from xxx that Bennett is inviting the audience to consider xxx.
- Here, the audience may well feel that Bennett is suggesting xxx.

Writing in an appropriate style

Remember that you are expected to write in a suitable register. In other words, you need to use an appropriate style. This means:

- *Not* using colloquial language or slang, e.g. 'The Head is a nasty piece of work. A bit too full of himself for my liking.' (The only exception is when quoting from the text.)

- *Not* becoming too personal, e.g. 'Rudge is like my mate, right, 'cos he…'.
- Using suitable phrases for an academic essay, e.g. 'It could be argued that', not 'I reckon that…'.
- *Not* being too dogmatic. Don't say 'This means that…'. It is much better to say 'This might suggest that…'.

You are also expected to be able to use a range of technical terms correctly. However, if you can't remember the correct name for a technique but can still describe it, you should still go ahead and do so.

> **GRADE** *BOOSTER*
>
> The examiners will expect you to use the appropriate terminology where you can. However, if you can't decide whether a phrase is a simile or a metaphor, it helps to just refer to it as an example of imagery.

The first person ('I')

It is perfectly appropriate to say 'I feel' or 'I think', especially if you are being asked for your opinion. Just remember that you are being asked for your opinion about what Bennett may have been trying to convey in his play (his themes and ideas) and how he does this (through characters, events, language, form and structure of the play).

Spelling, punctuation and grammar (AO4)

Remember that your spelling, punctuation and grammar are specifically targeted for assessment on this part of the examination, so take care with accuracy and don't be sloppy. If the examiner cannot understand what you are trying to say, he/she will not be able to give you credit for it.

> **GRADE** *BOOSTER*
>
> It is important to make the individual quotations you select brief and to try to embed them. This will save you time, enabling you to develop your points at greater depth and so raise your grade.

How to raise your grade

The most important advice is to answer the question which is in front of you, and you need to start doing this straight away. When writing essays in other subjects, you may have been taught to write a lengthy, elegant introduction explaining what you are about to do. You have only a short time in the Literature examination so it is best to get started as soon as you have gathered your thoughts together and made a brief plan.

Students often ask how long their answer should be. It is difficult to give a definitive answer because clearly candidates have different sized handwriting, but quality is always more important than quantity. A strongly focused answer of 2–3 sides which hits the criteria in the mark scheme will be rewarded at the very highest level. Conversely, if a response is 6–7 sides long but is not focused on the question, it will not receive many marks at all.

Sometimes students go into panic mode because they do not know how to start. The best advice is to get straight to the point, especially if you are answering an extract-based question (WJEC Eduqas). If you are responding to an extract, begin by picking out interesting words and phrases and unpicking or exploring them within the context or focus of the question. For example, if the question is about the way that education is presented, you need to focus on picking out words and phrases to do with education.

If you are responding to a more traditional essay-style question (AQA) it is still important to get quickly to the point. There is no point in simply rewriting the question. If a question asks about how Irwin is presented in the play, it is perfectly fine to begin: 'Bennett presents Irwin as…'.

No matter which of the exam boards you are following, it is crucial that you deal effectively with the methods used by the writer, in this case Bennett, and the effects created. Ask yourself, what methods has the writer used? Although there are a whole range of methods with which you need to be familiar, it might be something as simple as a powerful adjective. What do you think is the impact of that word? It might be that the word you are referring to has more than one meaning. If that is the case, the examiner will be impressed if you can discuss what the word means to you, but can also suggest other connotations the word may have.

Is there an actual overall effect? For instance, you may have noticed Bennett often uses dialogue which is extremely precise, eloquent and witty, so as well as analysing individual words or phrases (not necessarily all of them, just the most interesting ones) you could also describe the cumulative effect.

Remember that if you are following the AQA specification your knowledge of context (AO3) is also assessed. If you were writing about the way Bennett presents Hector you might wish to consider whether Hector's behaviour may have been viewed differently in the 1980s compared with today.

Be very careful to avoid lapsing into narrative. If you are asked about how Bennett presents Mrs Lintott, remember that the focus of the question is about the methods that Bennett uses. Do not simply tell the examiner what Mrs Lintott does or what she is like; this is a very common mistake.

If you are entered for WJEC Eduqas you also have to deal with the focus of the question in the play as a whole. You will be penalised if you do not do this so you MUST leave time. If you feel you may have more to offer on the extract but are concerned about the time, leave a space so that you can return to it if time allows.

Key points to remember

- Do not just jump straight in. Spending time wisely in those first moments may gain you extra marks later.
- Write a brief plan.
- Remember to answer all parts of the question.
- Use your time wisely. Try to leave a few minutes to look back over your work and check your spelling, punctuation and grammar, so that your meaning is clear and so that you know you have done the very best that you can.
- Keep an eye on the clock.

Grade 5 candidates

- Have a clear focus on the text and the task and make sure you are able to 'read between the lines'.
- Develop a clear understanding of the ways in which writers use language, form and structure to create effects for the readers.
- Use a range of detailed textual evidence to support comments.
- Use understanding of the idea that both writers and readers may be influenced by where, when and why a text is produced.

Grade 8 candidates

- Produce a consistently convincing, informed response to a range of meanings and ideas within the text.
- Use ideas that are well linked and will often build on one another.
- Dig deep into the text, examining, exploring and evaluating writers' use of language, form and structure.
- Carefully select finely judged textual references which are well integrated in order to support and develop responses to texts.
- Show perceptive understanding of how contexts shape texts and responses to texts.

Achieving a Grade 9

To reach the very highest level you need to have thought about the play more deeply and produce a response which is conceptualised, critical and exploratory at a deeper level. You might, for instance, challenge accepted critical views in evaluating whether the writer has always been successful. If, for example, you think Bennett has set out to criticise the way history is presented in the media, how successful do you think he has been?

REVIEW YOUR LEARNING

1   On which paper will you find *The History Boys* question?
2   Can you take your copy of the play into the exam?
3   Will you have a choice of questions?
4   How long do you have to answer the question?
5   What advice would you give to another student about using quotations?
6   Will you be assessed on spelling, punctuation and grammar in your response to *The History Boys*?
7   Why is it important to plan your answer?
8   What should you do if you finish ahead of time?
Answers on p. 104.

All GCSE examinations are pinned to specific areas of learning that the examiners want to be sure the candidates have mastered. These are known as Assessment Objectives or AOs. If you are studying *The History Boys* as an examination text for AQA or WJEC Eduqas, the examiner marking your exam response will be trying to give you marks, using the particular mark scheme for that board. However, all mark schemes are based on fulfilling the key AOs for English Literature.

Assessment Objectives

The Assessment Objectives that apply to your response to *The History Boys* depend on the exam board.

AQA and WJEC Eduqas

AO1	**Read, understand and respond to texts.** Students should be able to: • maintain a critical style and develop an informed personal response • use textual references, including quotations, to support and illustrate interpretations
AO2	**Analyse the language, form and structure used by a writer to create meanings and effects, using relevant subject terminology where appropriate.**
AO4	**Use a range of vocabulary and sentence structures for clarity, purpose and effect, with accurate spelling and punctuation.**

AQA only

AO3	**Show understanding of the relationship between texts and the contexts in which they were written.**

Skills

Let's break the Assessment Objectives down to see what they really mean.

AO1

> **AO1 Read, understand and respond to texts.**
> Students should be able to:
> - maintain a critical style and develop an informed personal response
> - use textual references, including quotations, to support and illustrate interpretations

At its most basic level, this AO is about having a good grasp of what a text is about and being able to express an opinion about it within the context of the question. For example, if you were to say: 'The play concerns an eccentric teacher called Hector' you would be beginning to address AO1 because you have made a personal response. An 'informed' response refers to the basis on which you make that judgement. In other words, you need to show that you know the play well enough to answer the question.

It is closely linked to the idea that you are also required to '**use textual references including quotations to support and illustrate interpretations**'. This means giving short direct quotations from the text. For example, if you wanted to support the idea that Hector's teaching methods could be unusual, you could use a direct quote to point to the fact that his classroom door is said to be '...locked against the Forces of Progress...' (p. 36). Alternatively, you can simply refer to details in the text, in order to support your views. So you might say: 'Hector is an eccentric teacher as is shown by the fact that he always locks his classroom door.'

Generally speaking, most candidates find AO1 relatively easy. Usually, it is tackled well — if you answer the question you are asked, this Assessment Objective will probably take care of itself.

AO2

> **AO2 Analyse the language, form and structure used by a writer to create meanings and effects, using relevant subject terminology where appropriate.**

AO2 is a different matter. Most examiners would probably agree that covering AO2 is a weakness for many candidates, particularly those students who only ever talk about the characters as if they were real people.

In simple terms, AO2 refers to the writer's methods and is often signposted in questions by the word 'how' or the phrase 'how does the writer present...'.

Overall AO2 is equal in importance to AO1, so it is vital that you are fully aware of this objective. '**Language**' refers to Bennett's use of words. Remember that writers choose words very carefully in order to achieve particular effects. They may spend quite a long time deciding between two or three words which are similar in meaning in order to create just the precise effect that they are looking for.

If you are addressing AO2 in your response to *The History Boys*, you will typically find yourself using Bennett's name and exploring the choices he has made.

For example, Bennett has Irwin using the phrase 'mists up the windows' in the opening speech of the play. Explaining why this phrase is apt for Irwin's character and suggesting how the audience might respond to it would certainly address AO2. To simply identify the phrase as a metaphor will gain little reward.

Language also encompasses a wide range of writer's methods, such as the use of different types of imagery, taboo language, litotes, irony and so on. AO2 also refers to your use of '**subject terminology**'. This means that you should be able to use terms such as 'metaphor', 'alliteration' and 'irony' with confidence and understanding. However, if you can't remember the term, don't despair — you will still gain marks for explaining the effects being created.

The terms '**form**' and '**structure**' refer to the kind of text you are studying and how it has been 'put together' by the writer. Obviously, Bennett wrote *The History Boys* as a stage play, so you should be aware of his use of stage directions and techniques such as the 'flash-forwards' that are used to open each Act. Structure might also include the way key events are juxtaposed, such as Hector's lessons compared with Irwin's.

Remember: if you do not address AO2 at all, it will be very difficult to achieve much higher than Grade 1, since you will not be answering the question.

AO3 (AQA only)

> **AO3** **Show understanding of the relationship between texts and the contexts in which they were written.**

Although AO3 is perhaps not considered as important as AO1 and AO2, it is still worth between 15% and 20% of your total mark in the AQA examination as a whole, and so should not be underestimated. Do remember that it is not assessed for this play if you are entered for WJEC Eduqas.

To cover AO3 you must show that you understand the links between a text and when, why and for whom it was written. For example, some awareness of the British education system in the 1980s may help you to understand Bennett's intentions in writing *The History Boys*. Equally, some knowledge of Bennett's background might give you useful insight into the way characters such as Posner are presented.

However, it is important to understand that context should not be 'bolted on' to your response for no good reason; you are writing about literature not history or biography.

AO4

> **AO4** Use a range of vocabulary and sentence structures for clarity, purpose and effect, with accurate spelling and punctuation.

This AO is fairly self-explanatory. A clear and well-written response should always be your aim. If your spelling is so bad or your grammar and lack of punctuation so confusing that the examiner cannot understand what you are trying to express, this will obviously adversely affect your mark.

Similarly, although there are no marks awarded for good handwriting, and none taken away for untidiness or crossings out, it is obviously important for the examiner to be able to read what you have written. If you believe your handwriting is so illegible that it may cause difficulties for the examiner, you need to speak to your school's examination officer in plenty of time before the exam. He/She may be able to arrange for you to have a scribe or to sit your examination using a computer.

What you will not gain many marks for

- **Retelling the story.** You can be sure that the examiner marking your response knows the story inside out. A key feature of the lowest grades is 'retelling the story'. Don't do it.

- **Quoting long passages**. Remember, the point is that every reference and piece of quotation must support a very specific point you are making. If you quote at length, the examiner will have to guess which bit of the quotation you mean to support your point. Don't impose work on the examiner — be explicit about exactly which words you have found specific meaning in. Keep quotes short and smart.

- **Merely identifying literary devices.** You will never gain marks simply for identifying literary devices such as a simile or a use of alliteration. However, you can gain marks by identifying these features, exploring the reasons why you think the author has used them and offering a thoughtful consideration of how they might impact on readers, as well as an evaluation of how effective you think they are.

- **Giving unsubstantiated opinions.** The examiner will be keen to give you marks for your opinions, but only if they are supported by reasoned argument and references to the text.
- **Writing about characters as if they are real people.** It is important to remember that characters are constructs — the writer is responsible for what the characters do and say. Don't ignore the author!

REVIEW YOUR LEARNING

1 What does AO1 assess?
2 What sort of material do you need to cover in order to successfully address AO2?
3 What do you understand by the term AO3?
4 What is meant by AO4?
5 Which exam board specification are you following and what AOs should you be focusing on?
6 What should you *not* do in your responses?

Answers on p. 104.

The question below is typical of an AQA question.

How does Bennett use the character of Irwin to explore ideas about education?

Write about:
- how Bennett presents the character of Irwin
- how Bennett uses Irwin to explore ideas about education.

[30 marks]

AO4 [4 marks]

Student X, who is expected to achieve a Grade 5, began the response like this:

1 Rather a sweeping statement which oversimplifies the issue.

Bennett's presentation of the character of Irwin is very negative. In the very first scene of the play he is presented as a successful spin doctor, advising some MPs on how to fool the public. So Bennett has given us a first impression of a man who is not to be trusted. When he first arrives at the school, Scripps remarks to the audience that there was something 'furtive' about him, so the audience has their first impression confirmed.

2 Some simple identification of effect.

As well as that early negative impression, he is contrasted to Hector who is the total opposite. Hector believes in what he is saying and the boys love him and this makes Irwin seem very shallow and superficial. The boys don't like him either because he tries 'to get down with the kids' when he starts discussing foreskins with them in their first lesson.

3 Fair point but needs explaining.

4 Avoid generalisations. Which boys exactly?

At this stage, this response seems more like a Grade 3. There is some focus on the task but little in terms of detail and explanation. The answer so far feels oversimplified and relies on generalisations.

Compare those two paragraphs with the following opening paragraphs by **Student Y** who is aiming to achieve a Grade 8.

1 Immediate focus on the task and clear awareness of a writer at work.

2 Well chosen, embedded textual detail.

> Bennett uses Irwin as a framing device at the start of the play and in the process establishes his character as that of a devious and cynical manipulator of the truth. He is seen operating as the often despised modern figure of the 'spin doctor'. By presenting him as a man who 'mists up the windows' of truth, Bennett ensures that the audience will have their doubts about Irwin when he first appears at the school, especially as he is described by Scripps as 'furtive'.
>
> Irwin's initial exchange with the Headmaster reveals his purpose to the audience: he is being employed solely to achieve success for the boys in their Oxbridge exams by adding what the Head describes as 'polish'. By placing this scene immediately after the audience's first encounter with the eccentric Hector, who despises the idea of his boys being prepared for Oxbridge, Bennett cleverly sets up the future conflict between the two teachers' attitudes to education.

3 Understands the effect created by the writer.

4 Begins to analyse an effect of structure.

These two paragraphs are clear and well focused, with some thoughtful consideration of Bennett's methods. The candidate has already revealed Grade 5 skills.

Both students now address Irwin's methods as a teacher. Look carefully at the differences in their responses in the following paragraphs.

Student X writes:

1 Detail linked to Irwin. Very brief quotation is a good idea.

> Irwin has a 'trick' which he wants to teach the boys to give them a better chance of getting into Oxford or Cambridge. In his first lesson Irwin throws back the boys' books and tells them that their essays are 'dull' and will not impress the Oxbridge examiners. His method is to teach the boys to approach topics from an unexpected angle so that their answers will stand out. For example, he suggests that they look for positive things to say about Stalin and argue that the British caused the First World War rather than accepting the more traditional view.
>
> When the boys argue that this is not true, Irwin says: 'What has that got to do with it?' By this statement Bennett is suggesting that education is going downhill because teaching history should be about the truth and the facts, as it is taught by Mrs Lintott, who was the boys' teacher at A-level.

2 Clear supporting details from the play — paraphrasing is fine.

3 Direct quotation followed by explanation linked to writer.

4 Oversimplification here. After all, Irwin's method does bring success. Always look for alternative interpretations.

Student X's response is improving at this stage with a greater level of detail and support. AO2 is still weak though – there is reference to Bennett's possible intentions but it is not really a clear understanding.

Now consider **Student Y's** approach to the same kind of material:

1 Thoughtful point revealing Irwin's contrast with Mrs Lintott.

In his first meeting with the boys, Irwin is dismissive of their work, describing it as competent but 'Abysmally dull', a criticism which effectively dismisses Mrs Lintott's more factual approach. Irwin believes the boys have no chance of competing for Oxbridge places against the public school students he calls 'thoroughbreds', unless they take on his method to make their work stand out from the pack. Bennett's use of the word 'thoroughbreds' and its link to racehorses and horse racing emphasises Irwin's competitive approach to education, perhaps also implying that the boys are like animals that can be trained to perform.

Irwin's 'angle' is to approach topics from an unexpected direction regardless of the accepted 'truth'. For example, he suggests that they argue that the British caused the First World War and that General Haig, far from being a 'butcher', actually 'delivered the goods'. Irwin is presented by Bennett as having little regard for the truth, which might appear negative to the audience, but his methods are later shown to be successful in that all the boys gain Oxbridge places. This poses an interesting question for the audience: which of Irwin or Hector would you rather taught your children?

2 Textual support well used.

3 Thoughtful and considered response to Bennett's use of language and its effects.

4 Close detail, well embedded quotations.

5 Offering alternative views of Irwin and his approach.

6 An interesting approach here suggesting a thoughtful approach to the issues.

In considering Irwin's approach to teaching, both students cover similar ground in their two paragraphs. However, it is obvious that Student Y has a more detailed approach and offers more thoughtful and varied interpretations expressed in a suitably tentative style using words such as 'might' and 'perhaps'. Student X has a specific interpretation of the play and puts this across in a clear, direct way but without considering the subtleties of the play and its characters.

Both students now consider the presentation of Irwin in the shared lesson with Hector in Act Two, an excellent section to consider as here the audience is shown how Irwin's ideas about education contrast with those of his older, more eccentric colleague.

Student X writes:

1 Clear understanding of the effect of Bennett's use of structure and good use of appropriate terminology.

2 Good to see an awareness of audience here.

> In the shared lesson in Act 2 Bennett juxtaposes Hector and Irwin's different views of education, allowing the audience to see their contrasting attitudes. At first it is obviously uncomfortable for them as they don't know how to start the lesson, but once the topic of the Holocaust comes up the audience is shown how different the two men are.
>
> Irwin encourages the boys to 'Distance yourselves' when dealing with this horrific topic and Bennett seems to be suggesting that Irwin sees the Holocaust as just another opportunity for impressing in an exam. This is in total contrast to Hector who is horrified by the idea that the Holocaust can be dealt with in this way. Most of the boys by this stage seem to be adapting to Irwin's ideas, especially Dakin, but when Posner, who is Jewish, reveals that he lost relatives in the Holocaust Irwin just says 'Good point' which suggests to the audience that he does not care about people's feelings as much as he cares about exam results.

3 Clear writer awareness — AO2 is being dealt with more effectively now.

4 Clearly explained idea which focuses on Irwin's ideas about education.

Student X's response is certainly improving. There is a definite sense of a clear understanding of what Irwin stands for and a growing confidence at dealing with the writer's methods. The response now feels like a secure Grade 5.

Student Y deals with the shared lesson as follows:

> The shared lesson in Act Two gives Bennett the opportunity to further reveal to the audience Irwin's ideas about education by juxtaposing them with the more traditional views of Hector. After an uncomfortable start for both teachers, the topic of the Holocaust is introduced and Irwin's distanced responses are contrasted powerfully with Hector's more emotional reactions. By using such a powerful and emotive topic as the Holocaust, Bennett is showing the audience just how far Irwin's relativist ideas can be taken. Irwin's advice to the boys to 'Distance yourselves' when dealing with this kind of horror reveals that Irwin sees the Holocaust as just another opportunity for impressing in an examination, a view that Bennett emphasises by Irwin's failure to understand Posner's more personal response.
>
> Irwin's rather unfeeling nature is further revealed by the total contrast to Hector who realises that Posner, who is Jewish, is '…speaking from the heart'. For Irwin, Posner's references to the members of his family who were lost in the Holocaust are reduced to the simple comment 'Good point'.
>
> Although many in the audience might find themselves in opposition to the apparent callousness of Irwin's ideas, it is noticeable that most of the boys have quickly adapted to his unusual approaches and understand how they may be used to gain success by avoiding what Lockwood describes as 'the stock answer'.

1 Good awareness of Bennett's use of structure to highlight ideas.

2 Impressive use of terminology and excellent understanding of Bennett's choice of subject matter.

3 Judicious use of textual support.

4 Interesting analysis — student is aware that there are no simple answers to these issues.

Student Y's detailed understanding of the issues of the play and sensitive responses to Bennett's methods are impressive. By this stage, a Grade 8 is certainly within sight.

Both students now consider Irwin's role in the 'mock interviews' before moving towards a conclusion. Again, this is a useful section of the play to select as it offers the audience an insight into Irwin's ideas while contrasting them with the views of both Hector and Mrs Lintott.

Student X writes:

> Irwin's ideas about education also come out very clearly when the three teachers conduct a mock interview with the boys to prepare them for what they might face at Oxford or Cambridge. Irwin's method for impressing at an interview is very different from Hector's as he once again is not interested in the truth. Irwin believes that the boys should not admit to liking Mozart, for example, because 'everyone likes Mozart'. Also, he advises Crowther not to mention his interest in acting because dons think it is a waste of time. In the interviews Bennett makes it clear that Irwin does not care about the truth but only that the boys stand out from the crowd. This shows us again how Irwin's ideas about education are all about competition and creating the right impression.
>
> Overall, Bennett presents Irwin as a man who is a manipulator and who cares more for success than he does for the truth. He has even lied about his own education to get a job! He believes examinations are a fact of life, unlike Hector, and I think Bennett wants the audience to see Irwin and his ideas as the future of education as Irwin replaces the Hectors of the teaching world.

1 Continuing focus on Irwin and 'ideas'.

2 Good textual detail — a clear grasp of the play and its events.

3 Clear conclusion but is it as simple as this? Could more be said on how the audience might view Irwin and his ideas?

Student X reaches a solid enough conclusion but it is a slight anti-climax. There would need to be further consideration of how Bennett might want the audience to view Irwin and his ideas if this response was to go beyond Grade 5.

Now read **Student Y's** closing paragraphs and see if you can understand why this candidate achieves a higher grade:

Bennett gives the audience further insight into Irwin's ideas about education in Act 2 when Irwin, Hector and Mrs Lintott conduct a mock interview with the boys to prepare them for what they are likely to face at Oxbridge. Irwin's technique for impressing at an interview is immediately apparent in his advice to Crowther to whom he says, 'Don't mention the theatre.' Irwin believes that the boys have to stand out from the rest of the interviewees and that this is best achieved by avoiding the truth, much to Hector's disgust: 'Why can they not all just tell the truth?'.

In the same way Irwin believes that the boys should not admit to liking Mozart, for example, because 'everyone likes Mozart' and he advises them instead to claim to prefer composers who are 'off the beaten track' such as Bruckner. In this way Bennett once more reveals to the audience that Irwin's ideas about education are all based on competition and creating a good impression, even at the expense of the truth. Interestingly, this is how we learn that Irwin lives his life, as he is shown to have lied to both the Headmaster and Dakin about having been educated at Oxford.

It would however be too easy to simply assume that Bennett wants his audience to disapprove of Irwin and his ideas about education. While he does seem to represent a new kind of teaching, he is shown to be successful in enabling lower middle-class boys to gain Oxbridge places, something Hector was unable to achieve. At the same time, by allowing the audience glimpses into the future, it could also be said that Bennett is concerned that Irwin's ideas will become the norm in the worlds of media and politics.

1 Focus remains on Irwin and ideas.

2 Detailed use of appropriate text.

3 Interesting detail linking ideas to Irwin's character.

4 Convincing conclusion showing a thorough understanding of the complexities of the play and Bennett's possible intentions.

Student Y has clearly covered all the criteria for a Grade 8, and the insights of the final paragraph probably lift the final grade to a 9.

You might notice that Student Y's response is not hugely longer than that of Student X. Quality is more important than quantity. A well-focused answer with appropriate detailed comments will always score higher than a rambling response which drifts from the point and touches briefly on many ideas, rather than exploring a few in depth.

The sample question below is typical of a WJEC Eduqas question.

> You should use the extract below and your knowledge of the whole play to answer this question.
>
> Write about the relationship between Hector and the boys and how it is presented at different points in the play.
>
> In your response you should:
>   - refer to the extract and the play as a whole;
>   - show your understanding of characters and events in the play. [40]

Five of this question's marks are allocated for accuracy in spelling, punctuation and the use of vocabulary and sentence structures.

Hector Hush, boys. Hush. Sometimes…sometimes you defeat me.

Dakin Oh no, sir. If we wanted to defeat you we would be like Cordelia and say nothing.

Hector Can't you see I'm not in the mood?

Dakin What mood is that, sir? The subjunctive? The mood of possibility? The mood of might-have-been?

Hector Get on with some work. Read.

Lockwood Read, sir? Oh come on, sir. That's no fun.

Akthar Boring.

Hector Am I fun? Is that what I am?

Timms Not today, sir. No fun at all.

Hector Is that what you think these lessons are? Fun?

Lockwood But fun is good, sir. You always say…

Posner Not just fun, sir.

Akthar (*pointing at Posner*) Would you like him to sing to you, sir? Would that help?

Hector Shut up! Just shut up. All of you. SHUT UP, you mindless fools. What made me piss my life away in this god-forsaken place? There's nothing of me left. Go away. Class dismissed. Go.

He puts his head down on the desk. There are some giggles and face-pullings before they realise it's serious. Now they're nonplussed and embarrassed. Scripps indicates to Dakin that Hector is crying. Scripps is nearest to him and ought to touch him, but doesn't, nor does Dakin. Posner is the one who comes and after some hesitation, pats Hector rather awkwardly on the back, saying, 'Sir.'

Student X, who is heading for a Grade 5, began his/her response like this:

1 No need to rephrase the question like this — much better to get straight to the point.

2 Fair comment but could be more appropriately expressed.

'The History Boys' is a play set in a school in Yorkshire and I will be writing about how the relationship between Hector and his class is presented in the extract and in the play as a whole. In the extract Hector is in a real low way because the Headmaster has found out about the motorbike 'incident' and has told him he must retire and this is shown by him saying that he is 'not in the mood'. The boys expect Hector's lessons to be enjoyable which is why they say that being told to read is 'no fun'. This shows that their relationship is usually a lively one as they are not used to seeing Hector behaving in this way.

3 Appropriate textual support and evidence of understanding the context of the extract.

4 A fairly simple but explained response to the relationship.

After a slow start, the response is beginning to focus on the extract and shows some understanding of the play's events. There is some support and explanation but, as yet, no sign of the writer's methods being considered.

Now compare that opening with this one by **Student Y**, who is working at a higher level:

1 Good to get straight to the point.

2 Good textual detail from outside the extract.

3 Concisely dealing with the immediate context of the extract.

4 Clear understanding of a method and its effect, and knowledge of the correct terminology.

5 Subtle point with regard to relationship between the boys and Hector.

> In the extract Hector is in what Bennett describes earlier in the scene as a 'sombre and distracted mood' due to the fact that the Headmaster has discovered the nature of Hector's exploits on his motorbike with the boys and has forced him to offer to retire otherwise he will be sacked. The tension in the extract is increased by Bennett's use of dramatic irony: at this point the audience fully understands why Hector is 'not in the mood' but the boys do not, as they believe his mood is linked to his being forced to share lessons with Irwin. The fact that Hector is attempting, albeit unsuccessfully, to tell the boys the truth about his situation suggests the mutual trust in their relationship.

This is an impressive opening in that it quickly establishes an overview of the extract, shows good awareness of writer and audience, reveals detailed textual knowledge, and makes a relevant point on the relationship in a single paragraph. At this early stage an examiner would probably already have recognised this as a potentially high-achieving candidate.

In the next sections of their responses both students focus on the extract itself and discuss what it reveals about the relationship between Hector and the boys.

Student X writes:

The way that the boys talk to Hector in the extract shows that the relationship they have with him is fairly open as they talk back to him and argue despite the fact that he is in a bad mood and wants them to be quiet. Bennett also shows the audience that the boys want to impress Hector with what they have learned from him and this is revealed when Dakin makes a reference to Cordelia from 'King Lear' and also to the subjunctive tense which Hector teaches them in the French lesson at the start of the play. It seems that the boys want to make Hector feel better by showing off what he has taught them.

When Hector suddenly explodes at the end of the extract and starts to cry the boys are described in the stage directions as 'embarrassed' and don't know how to react. This suggests that their relationship is normally quite light-hearted because they don't know how to react to Hector when he is genuinely upset rather than putting on an act.

The relationship shown in the extract suggests that most of the boys are insensitive towards Hector and may just see him as a figure of fun rather than as a human being. However, Bennett presents Posner as a more sensitive boy who has a closer link with Hector as he says the teacher is 'Not just fun, sir' and tries to comfort him by patting him on the back.

1 Focus on relationship.

2 Clear knowledge of allusions in the play.

3 Reference to Bennett's methods linked to a relevant point.

4 Subtle point shows an understanding that the relationships are quite complex.

At this point this is more typical of a Grade 4 response. It does have a clear focus on the task. There is a sense of a clear understanding of the relationship, but, as yet, AO2 has not been addressed in any detail.

Now look at how **Student Y** tackles the extract:

The manner in which the boys react to Hector and his 'mood' in this extract reveals that the relationship they normally enjoy is far from the traditional teacher-student relationship as Bennett suggests by the way the boys talk back to him, expecting the lesson to be 'fun' despite the fact that their teacher is clearly in a bad mood and wants them to be quiet.

1 Sensitive response to the extract.

At the same time, Bennett also suggests to the audience that the boys, particularly Dakin, want to impress Hector with what they have learned from him and this is revealed when Dakin makes a reference to Cordelia from 'King Lear'. Bennett uses this allusion to indicate Dakin's intelligence, as well as Hector's effectiveness as a teacher, whilst also perhaps foreshadowing Hector's eventual demise.

2 Understands reasons and effects of Bennett's use of literary allusion.

Although it would be easy to see some of the boys' behaviour in this extract as disrespectful, Bennett still makes it clear that the boys care about Hector as is shown by Akthar suggesting that Posner should sing for him and Posner himself trying to console Hector by saying his lessons are more than 'just fun.'

3 Considered alternative interpretation.

When Hector finally breaks down in front of the boys towards the end of the extract, Bennett shows the audience the difficulties in the teacher-pupil relationship, describing the boys in the stage directions as 'nonplussed' and 'embarrassed.' This suggests that in their relationship the boys have perhaps never recognised Hector as a human being because they clearly do not know how to react to Hector when he is revealing genuine feelings rather than putting on his act of 'studied eccentricity.'

4 Excellent use of textual detail from much earlier in the play.

Student Y deals with the extract very effectively, showing an understanding of the complexities of the relationship and also the methods by which Bennett presents it.

Now both candidates turn to the requirement to explore the relationship between Hector and the boys as it is presented in the play 'as a whole'. Remember: without addressing this aspect of the question it would be very difficult to achieve above Grade 3.

Here is **Student X's** response to the relationship at 'different points in the play'. Sensibly, Student X chooses to focus on the early lessons in Act One and also on Hector's memorial service as these are aspects which show much about their relationship:

Bennett shows how close the relationship is between Hector and the boys right from the start of the play when the boys remove Hector's motorbike gear calling out the names for the gear in French. This makes Hector seem like a conquering hero that the boys have a high regard for. The first time we see them in a lesson the relationship is quite surprising as we see Hector hitting Timms on the head with a book and calling him a 'trollop'. However, Bennett shows us that this was not taken seriously when Timms stands out from the action and speaks to the audience directly telling them that the hitting was just a joke and 'We lapped it up'. By having Timms speak directly to the audience as an adult Bennett is able to show us the truth about the relationship.

1 Relevant detail from elsewhere in the play.

2 Clear response to Bennett's use of a dramatic technique.

The closeness of the relationship is also shown in the French lesson in which the boys act out a scene in a French brothel. As long as the boys use the correct French, Hector does not mind about the content of the lesson. Bennett shows how the boys protect Hector when the Headmaster and Irwin enter the room. The boys quickly change the scene to a war-time hospital to make sure Hector does not get in trouble.

3 Continued range of response to task.

Hector and the boys' relationship is also presented in a more troubling way when we learn that Hector interferes with the boys that he gives a lift to on his motorbike. Obviously a modern audience would find this behaviour shocking and immoral, but the boys are shown to tolerate what Hector does and just accept it as part of Hector's eccentric character.

4 Attempts to consider a difficult idea in the play.

In the end the strength of the relationship is shown very powerfully after Hector's death when the students remember him at the memorial service. The boys have fond memories of Hector with Scripps saying that his education was 'the only education worth having'. Although the boys achieved their places at Oxbridge mostly because of Irwin, it is clear that their relationship with Hector was much closer.

5 Sound concluding point on the relationship.

Overall, the key words an examiner might use for this response are 'clear' and 'sustained'. Focus is held on the task throughout and a wide knowledge of events is revealed from the play as a whole. For this reason, we can now say that this response deserves a Grade 5, and could easily move to Grade 6 with a little more attention to Bennett's methods and effects.

Student Y also looks at the early lessons and the memorial service but explores them in more detail:

1 Explains effect and links it to task convincingly.

2 Excellent use of appropriate supporting stage direction.

3 Thoughtful analysis of Bennett's methods as a playwright.

> The relationship as displayed in the extract is very different from what we see earlier in the play when Hector is presented as more of a performer than a human being. The audience's first sight of the boys and Hector is of Hector being divested of his motorbike gear by the boys who then name the parts in French and display them 'with a flourish'. This stylised opening presents Hector like a returning knight being helped off his steed by his grooms, suggesting a close bond between both parties.
>
> When Bennett first presents the relationship in a lesson it is unconventional to say the least! Hector is shown hitting Timms on the head with a book and verbally abusing him; however, Bennett makes it clear that this is part of an established routine and describes Hector's part in it as an 'elaborate pantomime', suggesting Hector as a performer and the boys as a willing audience. The fact that Hector's behaviour is not taken seriously is reinforced by Bennett using Timms to 'break the fourth wall' and address the audience directly, informing them in the past tense that the hitting was just a joke and that 'None of us cared. We lapped it up'.
>
> The mutual trust in the relationship is clearly shown in the French lesson in which the boys eagerly improvise a scene in a French brothel. Providing that the boys use the correct verb forms and tenses, Hector does not seem to be concerned about the content of the lesson. At the same time, Bennett shows how the boys protect Hector when the lesson is interrupted when the Headmaster and Irwin enter the room. The boys quickly change the scene to a war-time hospital to explain Dakin's lack of trousers to make sure Hector does not have to explain an awkward situation to the Headmaster. This trust is also revealed in a less comedic way when Irwin tries to extract information

about Hector's lessons from Posner who is clearly uncomfortable with this and avoids answering him.

4 Judicious choice of supporting detail.

Perhaps the aspect of the relationship that is most disturbing for a modern audience concerns Hector's sexual activities with some of the boys on his motorbike. Clearly his behaviour is unacceptable but curiously it does not seem to affect the boys' feelings towards him. The boys who regularly 'suffer' Hector's attentions, such as Dakin and Scripps, tolerate his behaviour as simply an element of his eccentricity. Furthermore, Bennett does not present either boy as in any way damaged by the experience; only Posner is shown to have problems later in life and he was never touched by Hector.

5 Clear, sensitive analysis of a difficult idea.

The positive nature of the boys' relationship with Hector is most movingly presented at the end of the play during Hector's memorial service. Lockwood declares that Hector made him realise that teachers were human beings and Akthar refers to the 'contract' that existed between Hector and his class. Above all, Scripps describes Hector as offering the 'only education worth having' which is a fitting tribute to the relationship between Hector and his boys.

6 Beautifully summed up final paragraph.

Student Y's response is thoughtful and convincing, showing a detailed knowledge of characters and events and a considered approach to Bennett's methods and effects. Grade 8 would be comfortably awarded to a response of this standard.

GRADE **BOOSTER**

Now attempt your own answer to the appropriate question for the examination board whose specification you are following and practise writing to the time limit.

As your examination will be 'closed book', you might find it helpful to memorise some quotations to use in support of your points in the examination response. Turn to the 'Tackling the exams' section on pp. 66–74 for further information about the format of the examination.

In the section below you will find quotations relating to the key moments in the action of the play, the main characters and the themes, as well as an indication of why each quotation is important.

You don't need to remember long quotations; short quotes that you can embed into a sentence will be more effective. There are a number of different techniques to help you memorise quotations, some of which appear in the Grade boosters in this section. Some students find learning quotations easier than others. However, if all else fails, as long as you can remember the gist of what the quotation relates to, you could use a textual reference instead.

GRADE *BOOSTER*

```
The most frequently used method for learning quotations
is to write them down, repeat them and then test
yourself. However, if you are a visual learner, you
might try drawing one of these 'moments' with the
quotation as a caption.
```

Key moments

The following quotations provide you with a 30-second version of the entire play.

1

Headmaster Factually tip-top as your boys always are, something more is required. (p. 8)

- This reveals the Headmaster's superficiality as he explains to Mrs Lintott that he needs to bring someone in to add polish.

2

Hector Child, I am your teacher. Whatever I do in this room is a token of my trust. (p. 6)

- The bond between Hector and the boys is established.

3

Irwin History nowadays is not a matter of conviction. It's a performance. It's entertainment. And if it isn't, make it so. (p. 35)

- This displays Irwin's populist views on history.

Headmaster A hand on a boy's genitals at fifty miles an hour, and you call it nothing? (p. 53)

4

- This expresses the Headmaster's outrage as Hector is unable to see he has done anything wrong.

Hector What made me piss my life away in this god-forsaken place? (p. 65)

5

- This shows that Hector is in despair, despite his brave face in the Headmaster's office.

Hector But how can you teach the Holocaust? (p. 70)

6

- This reveals how Hector is more sensitive and compassionate than Irwin.

Irwin No. But this is history. Distance yourselves. (p. 74)

7

- This demonstrates how different Irwin is from Hector and shows that he is even prepared to use something as horrific as the Holocaust to his own ends.

Headmaster Splendid news! Posner a scholarship, Dakin an exhibition and places for everyone else. (p. 97)

8

- This shows the audience that Irwin's methods have been successful.

Scripps And here history rattled over the points... (p. 105)

9

- Supporting Bennett's views on the random nature of history, this is the moment when everything changes.

Hector Pass it on boys. That's the game I wanted you to learn. Pass it on. (p. 109)

10

- This encapsulates Hector's educational philosophy.

Top character quotations
Irwin

'Paradox works well and mists up the windows, which is handy. "The loss of liberty is the price we pay for freedom" type of thing.' (p. 1)

1

- An important comment as its sums up Irwin's cynical view about the nature of truth.

2

'Poetry is good up to a point. Adds flavour.' (p. 26)
- Encapsulates Irwin's cynical views on literature and is in complete contrast to Hector's approach. For Irwin, knowledge is a means to an end.

3

'...truth is no more at issue in an examination than thirst at a wine-tasting or fashion at a striptease.' (p. 26)
- Demonstrates Irwin's approach to exams and education as a game.

Hector

4

'The best moments in reading are when you come across something — a thought, a feeling, a way of looking at things — which you had thought special and particular to you.' (p. 56)
- Reveals Hector's sincere belief in the importance of literature.

5

'Why can they not all just tell the truth?' (p. 83)
- Demonstrates Hector's rejection of Irwin's gamesmanship in the coaching of the boys prior to their interviews.

6

'I didn't actually do anything. It was a laying-on of hands, I don't deny that, but more in benediction than gratification or anything else.' (p. 95)
- Suggests that Hector fails to understand that he has done anything wrong.

Mrs Lintott

7

'Plainly stated and properly organised facts need no presentation, surely.' (p. 9)
- Explains Mrs Lintott's factual approach to history.

8

'History is a commentary on the various and continuing incapabilities of men.' (p. 85)
- Important as an example of Mrs Lintott's feminist views.

Headmaster

9

'Think charm. Think polish. Think Renaissance Man.' (p. 9)
- Reveals the Headmaster's superficial approach to education.

Posner

[quoting from *King Lear*] '...Speak what we feel, not what we ought to say.' (p. 7)

10

- Suggests his support for Hector's brand of education.

Top theme quotations
History

Rudge It's just one fucking thing after another. (p. 85)

1

- This reveals Rudge's simple but comedic view of history.

Mrs Lintott History is women following behind with the bucket. (p. 85)

2

- Mrs Lintott's view of the male-dominated nature of history.

Irwin But this is history. Distance yourselves. (p. 74)

3

- A summation of Irwin's dispassionate stance on historical events, including the Holocaust.

Education

Hector [quoting A. E. Housman] 'All knowledge is precious whether or not it serves the slightest human use'... (p. 5)

4

- A good demonstration of Hector's attitudes to education.

Irwin You can write down, Rudge, that 'I must not write down every word that teacher says.' (p. 26)

5

- This stresses Irwin's view on the need for originality in exams.

6   **Headmaster** Otherwise all bright but they need polish. Edge. (p. 11)
- This indicates the Headmaster's shallow take on education.

7   **Irwin** Education isn't something for when they're old and grey and sitting by the fire. It's for now. (p. 49)
- Irwin's view contrasts with Hector's anti-examination viewpoint.

GRADE *BOOSTER*

```
You may have a favourite quotation which is not listed
here and which you feel may be useful to support an
idea about the play. Add it to the appropriate list
and memorise it.
```

Sex and sexuality

8   **Dakin** She's my Western Front. Last night, for instance, meeting only token resistance, I reconnoitred the ground. (p. 28)
- This demonstrates that Dakin sees Fiona as territory to be conquered rather than as a person and that he is keen to share these details with Scripps.

9   **Hector** See it as an inoculation, rather. Briefly painful but providing immunity for however long it takes. With the occasional booster...another face, a reminder of the pain...it can last you half a lifetime. (p. 94)
- A revelation of the sadness behind Hector's suppressed desires.

10   **Mrs Lintott** A husband on a low light, that's what they want, these supposedly unsuspecting wives, the man's lukewarm attentions just what they married them for. (p. 92)
- This displays Mrs Lintott's somewhat cynical view of marriage.

GRADE *BOOSTER*

```
Another useful method to memorise quotatations is to
record them onto your MP3 player and play them over
and over. Or you might try watching the film to spot
where a quote appears. This can be an effective method
as you have both sound and vision to help you, and you
can see it in context. However, don't forget that there
are some significant differences between the film and
the stage play and that in your examination you are
answering on the stage play. Don't get them confused!
```

Other works by Alan Bennett

- *Forty Years On* (in *Alan Bennett: Plays*) (Faber and Faber, 1996): an earlier work set in a boys' public school which takes the form of a play that the boys are putting on for the parents. It deals with the loss of innocence after the First World War.
- Any of the plays from the *Talking Heads* series.
- *A Life like Other People's* (Faber, 2009): a highly readable autobiography dealing with Bennett's early life, his parents' marriage and relations with his extended family.

Poetry

It would be useful to read some First World War poetry. 'The Soldier' by Rupert Brooke is referenced by Posner as being similar in sentiment to 'Drummer Hodge', although Hector feels it to be not as good as the Hardy poem. If you are following the WJEC Eduqas specification, you will find a copy of this poem in the Eduqas anthology. The poetry of Wilfred Owen, particularly 'Exposure', which is in the Power and Conflict section of the AQA poetry anthology, and 'Dulce et Decorum Est', which is in the WJEC Eduqas anthology, plus Siegfried Sassoon's war poems, are also worth reading.

History

The First World War is in many ways seen as a turning point in history. Your history department at school or college may be the best place to find out more about the causes of the First World War to help you assess Irwin's viewpoint. You could also look at *The War that Ended Peace* (Profile Books, 2014) by Margaret MacMillan.

Context (p. 14)

1 The historical, socioeconomic and political setting of the play. May also refer to the literary context.
2 Sheer vanity plus love for another young man who was going there.
3 He used similar methods to gain academic success.
4 Dakin.
5 The play was set in the 1980s and first premièred in 2004.
6 The national curriculum and the publication of league tables.
7 21.
8 Because of Section 28 which outlawed any teaching which might be considered to promote homosexuality.
9 'Breaking the fourth wall' is a technique which disrupts the feeling of realism and reminds the audience that they are watching a play, such as an actor speaking directly to the audience.
10 Irwin as spin doctor at the beginning of Act One; Irwin as television historian at the start of Act Two.

Plot and structure (p. 29)

1 To add 'polish' and boost the boys' Oxbridge chances.
2 A brothel.
3 'Bewitched, Bothered and Bewildered'.
4 It is locked against the 'Forces of Progress'/'the future'/he doesn't like to be interrupted.
5 Posner tells Irwin that he thinks he may be homosexual.
6 The Headmaster's wife, Mrs Armstrong.
7 Hector puts out his hand and Posner almost takes it or they share an understanding of the power of poetry.
8 The Headmaster demands it as he is concerned about Hector's possible behaviour.
9 They have an accident in which Hector is killed and Irwin seriously injured.
10 He lives alone in a cottage/has 'periodic breakdowns'/his only friends are online.

Characterisation (p. 40)

1 The Headmaster calls Hector a 'loose cannon'.
2 Hector thinks examinations are the enemies of education.
3 Relativism is the idea that there's no such thing as truth, so that all points of view are equally valid.
4 She believes in the importance of well-ordered facts.
5 By his sexual harassment of his secretary, Fiona.
6 A tax lawyer.
7 His reward to Posner is a brief hug/he is put off Irwin by his wheelchair.
8 In order to impress Dakin.
9 He addresses the audience directly.
10 He is seen as an 'oddity' who has 'No hope'.

Themes (p. 51)

1 It will help them deal with life.
2 He calls them 'Cheat's Visas'.
3 'Drummer Hodge' by Thomas Hardy.
4 Scripps.
5 The Headmaster's wife did not normally work in the charity shop on Wednesdays. If a customer had come in or the lights had changed, she might not have seen the incident.
6 She reminds them that one of the dons could be a woman.
7 Dakin blackmails the Headmaster by telling him that he knows about his harassment of Fiona.
8 He went off to Dumfries.
9 Posner.
10 Philip Larkin's 'MCMXIV'.

Language, style and analysis (p. 65)

1 A minimal set encourages the audience to focus on the words/makes the play 'timeless'.
2 A bow-tie.
3 He uses the past tense.
4 We see them as typical teenagers. This emphasises their vulnerability.
5 She 'breaks the fourth wall', speaking directly to the audience.
6 She calls Hector a 'twerp'.
7 Ordinary 'realistic' speech'.

8 Irwin is false and showy.

9 Intertextuality is the referencing in one text to a different text. It is designed to enrich your understanding of the first text.

10 The metaphor Dakin uses is from warfare or invasion.

Tackling the exams (p. 74)

1 Paper 2.

2 No.

3 Yes for AQA, no for WJEC Eduqas.

4 Approximately 45 minutes.

5 Keep them brief and try to embed them into your writing.

6 Yes.

7 To help you avoid repeating yourself or getting into a muddle, and to enable you to gather your thoughts.

8 Check your work.

Assessment Objectives and skills (p. 79)

1 Your understanding of the text and your ability to support your ideas.

2 You need to explain how the writer uses language, form and structure to create effects.

3 AO3 refers to your understanding of the relationship between texts and the contexts in which they were written.

4 Spelling, punctuation and grammar.

5 For AQA, AO1, AO2, AO3 and AO4. For WJEC Eduqas AO1, AO2 and AO4.

6 You should not retell the story, quote at length, simply identify devices without explaining their effects, offer unsupported opinions, or write about characters as if they were real. Remember to avoid these and you won't go far wrong!